An Illustrated Guide to Jack the Ripper

Spitalfields & Whitechapel in 1888

AN ILLUSTRATED GUIDE TO

JACK THE RIPPER

TEXT BY PETER FISHER
FOREWORD BY ROBIN ODELL

First Published 1996

Published by P & D Riley
12 Bridgeway East
Runcorn
Cheshire
WA7 6LD
England

ISBN: 1 874712 26 3 (Hardcover)
ISBN: 1 874712 27 1 (Paperback)

British Library Cataloguing - in - Publication Data
A Catalogue Record for this book is available from the British Library

Typeset by AD Typesetting
Printed and bound in England by Redwood Books, Wiltshire, from artwork supplied

Acknowledgements

The author has been collecting information and illustrations about the Jack the Ripper crimes and Victorian London for more than 20 years and the number of people who have contributed, helped, listened to, and supported the venture have been in their hundreds, too many, in fact, to list here. But there have been certain supporters and friends who have to be mentioned. Grateful thanks must go to Robin Odell, the author of two works on Jack the Ripper (the second with Colin Wilson), who has contributed enormously to this book by supplying not only some of his personal collection of photographs and the Foreword, but also by supplying most of the Who's Who section, a task which would have made a wonderful book by itself in its entirety. Many thanks also to Stewart Evans, Richard Whittington-Egan, Paul Begg, Martin Fido, Peter Underwood, Patrick Moore, Chaim Bermant, the late Stephen Knight, the Rev. 'Eddy' Stride, Rector of Christ Church, Spitalfields in the 1970s, for allowing me unlimited access to parish registers for 1888, and to New Scotland Yard for supplying photographs, Whitechapel Library, Edward Tilley, Picture Librarian at The Public Records Office, London, the former Greater London County Council, Madame Tussauds, London, Dan Farson, Donald Rumbelow, Donna, Adam and Melanie Riley, the late Roy Bryan, Carol Whaley, the late Walter J. Arnold, Harry Turner, Radio Times Hulton Picture Library, *Times Newspapers*, the *Manchester Evening News*, the *Bolton Evening News*, *The Guardian*, the former *London Evening News*, June and Kenneth Bryan, Former BBC Radio Manchester (now GMR), presenters Jeff Cooper and Roy Cross.

Thanks also to John Morrison for supplying some of his enormous photographic collection, *The Sunday Times*, Dr. Barnardo's, Euston Films and Thames Television, Central Broadcasting, Scott Marshall Personal Management for the picture of Frank Windsor, *The Listener*, Sir Robert Mark, former Commissioner of the London Metropolitan Police, Mark Galloway of the Cloak and Dagger Club, BBC Television, Paul Acton and Dave Keen of the *East London Advertiser*, the *Illustrated London News*, Nick Warren of *Ripparana Magazine*, Russ Lawrence of the *Hackney Gazette*, Val Weeks of the *Waltham Forest Guardian*, Tibor Sever of *Books*, Llangollen, North Wales, the Jewish Historical Society, London, The Church of England Enquiry Centre, London, Keeper of the Archives, The University Library, Cambridge, Photorama of Earlestown, Lancashire, London Board of Shechita, London, and Yvette Laboy of New York.

To the many others who have also helped, but which space denies inclusion, or to anyone who has been inadvertently missed off this list, the author offers his sincere thanks for the help he has received. The author and publisher have also made every attempt over the years to trace the copyright owners of photographs, and in the event of failing to do so offer their apologies and will be pleased to rectify the discrepancy in any future edition.

Cover Photograph from: *The Black Museum.* (Central Broadcasting)

1888 : LEADING DATES

AUGUST 31   Mary Nichols murdered at Bucks Row

AUGUST 31   James Monro resigned as Assistant Commissioner of the Metropolitan
                     Police at New Scotland Yard

SEPTEMBER 8   Annie Chapman murdered in rear yard of 29 Hanbury Street

SEPTEMBER 10   John Pizer arrested as a murder suspect

SEPTEMBER 24   George Bernard Shaw, the dramatist, wrote a letter to The Star about 'Blood
                     Money'

SEPTEMBER 25   Letter signed *Jack the Ripper* sent to the Central News Agency.

SEPTEMBER 26   Coroner Wynne Baxter concluded inquest on Annie Chapman and referred to
                     the market for her missing organ.

SEPTEMBER 30   The *Double Event* when Elizabeth Stride and Catherine Eddowes were
                     murdered on the same night within 40 minutes of each other.

OCTOBER 1   Commissioner Sir Charles Warren attended trial of bloodhounds in Regents
                     Park - the dogs became lost in the London fog!

OCTOBER 16   George Lusk, Chairman of Whitechapel Vigilante Committee received letter
                     From Hell accompanied by a piece of human kidney.

OCTOBER 29   Dr. Openshaw received letter signed *Jack the Ripper*.

NOVEMBER 8   Sir Charles Warren resigned

NOVEMBER 9   Mary Kelly murdered at 13 Millers Court, Spitalfields.

NOVEMBER 12   Dr. Roderick MacDonald presided over swiftly concluded inquest into the
                     murder of Mary Jane Kelly.

NOVEMBER 12   George Hutchinson made a statement to the police describing a man he
                     saw with Mary Jane Kelly.

DECEMBER 3   James Monro appointed Commissioner of London Metropolitan Police in
                     succession to Sir Charles Warren

DECEMBER 26   Dr. Roslyn Donston Stephenson made a statement setting out his suspicions
                     that Dr. Morgan Davies was *Jack the Ripper*.

DECEMBER 31   Body of Montague John Druitt found floating in River Thames.

Foreword by
Robin Odell

Author of Jack the Ripper in Fact & Fiction

This is a subject whose perennial fascination is in danger of becoming swamped by the sheer weight of information and theorising which it generates. The published work on Jack the Ripper has reached encyclopaedic proportions and perhaps, like the Encyclopaedia Britannica, needs a macropaedia to guide the reader's interests. It is pleasing, therefore, to welcome Peter Fisher's initiative in producing *An Illustrated Guide to Jack the Ripper* which is a kind of macropaedia.

When a subject acquires such a wealth of theories and variety of conflicting interpretation, it is useful to read accounts that are not simply urging the reader to embrace some radically new belief. Such a work was Richard Whittington-Egan's *A Casebook on Jack the Ripper,* published in 1975, in which the author applied an objective critique to all that had gone before.

Paul Begg et al did much the same in their comprehensive *The Jack the Ripper A to Z,* published in 1991. This was for all practical purposes, the "Ripper encyclopaedia" and ranks as an outstanding reference book on the subject. This was followed in 1994 by Philip Sugden's *The Complete History of Jack the Ripper,* described, probably justifiably, by the publisher as the "definitive account". The book is well-researched and sensibly written, but requires over five hundred pages to take the reader through a story in which successive commentators in their desire to contribute something unique have succeeded in blurring the distinction between fact and fiction.

The facts about those momentous events in 1888 which may be regarded as irrefutable represent a small body of knowledge indeed. Recounting the brutal murders of five prostitutes within an area of less than a square mile of London's East End over a ten week period, can be fitted into a few pages. It is the accretions of theory and fantasy built up over the succeeding hundred and more years to explain them which require hundreds of pages of closely argued text.

By taking an essentially visual approach to his subject, Peter Fisher has recreated the environment in which Jack the Ripper lived, worked and killed. At the height of Britain's imperial power during the reign of Queen Victoria, the capital city contained within it a pocket of social degradation over which a veil had been conveniently drawn. The Whitechapel Murders changed that overnight by throwing a harsh spotlight on the appalling living conditions in the East End which began to gnaw at the consciences of many influential Victorians.

The area was over-populated, rife with crime, drunkenness and prostitution, under-policed and largely forgotten. Murder as a means of provoking social reform was probably not part of Jack the Ripper's agenda, but that was one of the effects. In this respect at least, the Whitechapel Murders were a catalyst for change. They were also a watershed in terms of the development of criminal behaviour. It has become fashionable to talk of Jack the Ripper as the first serial killer. That may or may not be relevant, but what is of greater significance is that he made the public aware in the the most brutal fashion possible, of the existence of the sex murder.

This had been hinted at in 1867 following the violent killing and butchery of eight year old Fanny Adams by William Baker. Such crimes of fiendish mutilation were easily branded as the work of homicidal maniacs. Although Jack the Ripper also earned that particular label in contemporary accounts, it became clear to the police that they were dealing with an individual who was alert, knowledgeable and wily in the extreme. Recognising that the human condition embraced some alienated individuals with a strong desire to mutilate and destroy which was not excusable as insanity; was as realistic as it was unwelcome.

The inability of the police to capture Jack the Ripper was in part due to the native cunning of their prey but also to their lack of investigative skills and the absence of scientific method. This was another facet of the murders that heralded change. Within a few years, fingerprint identification and microscopic examination would take the place of anthropometry and the magnifying glass as true aids to the scientific investigation of crime.

For all these reasons, Jack the Ripper occupies an unchallenged place in the annals of crime. But the abiding interest in the murders lies not in the reforms which they engendered but with the obsession to identify the killer. It is one of the principles of civilisation that every death of a human being shall be fully explained. It is also a deeply ingrained instinct that all mysteries shall be resolved. The list of possible identities for Jack the Ripper reads like a Demonic Roll Call. And it is a list without end, for no identification has yet been made with the power to command universal acceptance. Final, clinching evidence proves tantalisingly elusive. Nevertheless, legions of new researchers continue to probe the mysteries of England' s greatest murders in the hope of finding some hitherto neglected clue to identity.

There is little on this subject that can be said with certainty. But it is likely that Jack the Ripper was to all outward appearances a normal individual living and working in the cosmopolitan milieu of the East End. He knew the people. He knew the streets. He understood how to exploit the weaknesses of his victims. His fluency with the knife added potency to his destructive lusts. He sensed the ineffectiveness of his pursuers. All these factors conspired with an element of luck to protect him. Having defied over a hundred years of intense enquiry to unmask him, perhaps history should acknowledge that Jack the Ripper really did get away with murder.

Peter Fisher's **An Illustrated Guide to Jack the Ripper** *reminds us of the essentials of the Whitechapel Murders. It is not intended to be all-encompassing . It sets out to give a flavour of the streets, a picture of daily life and insights into the character of the people. It is a modest, but nonetheless rich, visual history of long-remembered infamous crimes and their social setting.*

Robin Odell

Hunt for a killer

The search for a killer is always time consuming which is either successful or disappointing, but few, if any, criminal investigations can be as time consuming, interesting, disappointing, or frustrating as the search for a killer who murdered at least five women more than a century ago and then made the world take notice for over 100 years by dubbing himself *Jack the Ripper*.

Seeking the Victorian maniac who slaughtered his victims in the East End of London districts of Whitechapel and Spitalfields in 1888 is as potent today among amateur detectives as it was among the most professional investigators all those years ago.

When Arthur Conan Doyle created the words..."life is infinitely stranger than anything which the mind of man could invent," for his character Sherlock Holmes in *A case of Identity*, he could have been writing about the strange life of Victorian Whitechapel.

And when he quoted Holmes as saying in *The Red Headed League* the words..."As a rule, the more bizarre a thing is the less mysterious it proves to be..." he could have been writing about Jack the Ripper. Far fetched? I believe not. Victorian Whitechapel was certainly a strange place filled with strange people as we will examine in detail, but it is as

The Duke of Clarence and his fianceé Princess May of Teck

well to point out here that I have always believed that the solution to Jack the Rippers killings (and even his identity) is far less mysterious than is generally supposed. I have never believed in the Montague John Druitt theory, or the alleged

9

THE PENNY ILLUSTRATED PAPER AND ILLUSTRATED TIMES

London. Printed and Published at the Office, 10, Milford-lane, Strand, in the Parish of St. Clement Danes, in the County of Middlesex, by Thomas Fox, 10, Milford-lane, Strand, afore

KATE EDDOWES THE MITRE SQUARE VICTIM

SKETCH OF THE MAN WHO VISITED MⁿLUSK

involvement of the Duke of Clarence and his high-powered flunkies; I have never suspected strange Russians or killers later hanged for using different *modus operandi*. There is little or no logic to these arguments. The answer, I believe, has always been relatively clear. Jack the Ripper was a part of the the community in which he slaughtered his prostitute victims. But more of this later, for I digress. It is important now to examine in detail the district in which 'Saucy Jack' plied his evil trade! Charles Booth, the Victorian statistician and reformer, who produced a mammoth documentary about 19th century poverty titled *Life and Labour of the People in London* gave an impression of the East End which is impossible to fault in its descriptive passages. It concisely portrays the mentality of a people long gone, but which still serves as a very important backcloth to the centre stage upon which played Jack the Ripper.

Under a sub-title *Sleeping in the Open Air* Booth wrote: "Sleeping out of doors is one of the features at Whitechapel. It is a centre for common lodging-houses and shelters. Destitutes from all sides are drawn there. Many would rather sleep out of doors than indoors in the warm weather. If they are without visual means of subsistence the police can charge them; if they have a few pence, as they generally have, they can only be moved from door to door, and finally will move no further and are left sleeping on the doorstep. They also sleep during the day on such seats as are provided. These people are covered with vermin and cannot be touched with impunity."

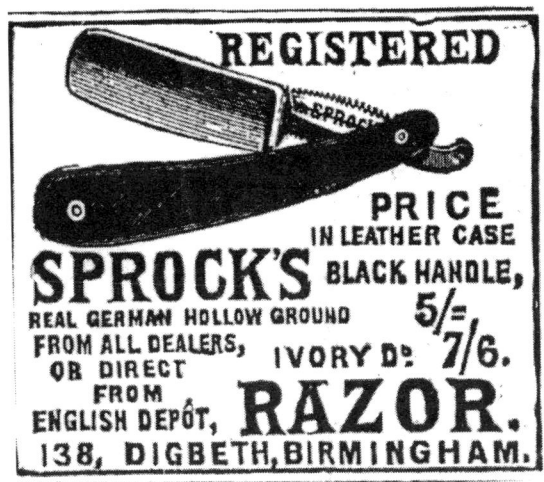

Trading Centre

He went on: "Whitechapel is the dwelling place of the Jews - tailors, bootmakers, and tobacco workers - and the centre of trading both small and large; Stepney and St George's the district of ordinary labour; Shoreditch and Bethnal Green of the artisan; in Popular sub-officials reach their maximum proportion, while Mile End, with a little of everything, very closely represents the average of the whole district; and finally Hackney stands apart with its well-to-do surburban population.

"Each district has its character-its peculiar flavour. One seems to be conscious of it in the streets. It may be in the faces of the people, or in what they carry - perhaps a reflection is thrown in this way from the prevailing trades - or it may lie in the sounds one hears, or in the character of the buildings."

Booth continued dramatically: "The feeling that I have just described - this excitement of life *which can accept murder as a dramatic incident,* (my italics) and drunkenness as the buffoonery of the stage - is especially characteristic of Whitechapel. And looked at in this way, what a drama it is!

"Whitechapel is a veritable Tom

Charles Booth

Tiddler's ground, the Eldorado of the East, a gathering together of poor fortune-seekers; its streets are full of buying and selling, the poor living on the poor. Here, just outside the old City walls, have always lived the Jews, and here they are now in thousands, both old-established and new comers, seeking their livelihood under conditions which seem to suit them on the middle ground between civilisation and barbarism. "The neighbourhood of old Petticoat Lane on Sunday is one of the wonders of London, a medley of strange sights, strange sounds, and strange smells. Streets crowded so as to be throughfares no longer, and lined with a double or treble row of hand-barrows, set fast with empty cases, so as to assume the guise of market stalls.

"Here and there a cast may have been drawn in, but the horse has gone and the tilt is used as a rostrum whence the salesmen with stentorian voices cry their wares, vying with each other in introducing to the surrounding crowd their cheap garments, smart braces, sham jewellery, or patent medicines. Those who have something showy, noisily push their trade, while the modest

Petticoat Lane in the 1880s

merit of the utterly cheap makes its silent appeal from the lower stalls, on which are to be found a heterogenous collection of such things as common sheeting, American cloth for the furniture covers, old clothes, worn out boots, damaged lamps, chipped china shepherdesses, rusty locks, and rubbish indescribable.

Buyer

"Other stalls supply daily wants-fish is sold in large quantities - vegetables and fruit - queer cakes and outlandish bread. In nearly all cases the Jew is the seller, and the Gentile the buyer: Petticoat Lane is the exchange of Jew, but the lounge of the Christian."

From his description of Petticoat Lane market, Booth went on to describe further the atmosphere of Whitechapel,

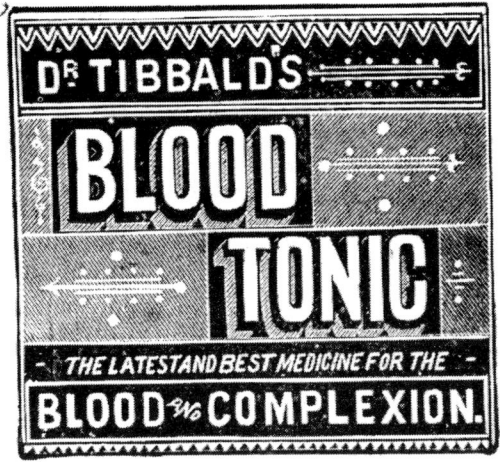

A group of Whitechapel orphans

A group of prostitutes in Whitechapel

GHASTLY MURDER

IN THE EAST-END.

DREADFUL MUTILATION OF A WOMAN.

Capture : Leather Apron

Another murder of a character even more diabolical than that perpetrated in Buck's Row, on Friday week, was discovered in the same neighbourhood, on Saturday morning. At about six o'clock a woman was found lying in a back yard at the foot of a passage leading to a lodging-house in a Old Brown's Lane, Spitalfields. The house is occupied by a Mrs. Richardson, who lets it out to lodgers, and the door which admits to this passage, at the foot of which lies the yard where the body was found, is always open for the convenience of lodgers. A lodger named Davis was going down to work at the time mentioned and found the woman lying on her back close to the flight of steps leading into the yard. Her throat was cut in a fearful manner. The woman's body had been completely ripped open, and the heart and other organs laying about the place, and portions of the entrails round the victim's neck. An excited crowd gathered in front of Mrs. Richardson's house and also round the mortuary in old Montague Street, whither the body was quickly conveyed. As the body lies in the rough coffin in which it has been placed in the mortuary —the same coffin in which the unfortunate Mrs. Nicholls was first placed—it presents a fearful sight. The body is that of a woman about 45 years of age. The height is exactly five feet. The complexion is fair, with wavy dark brown hair; the eyes are blue, and two lower teeth have been knocked out. The nose is rather large and prominent.

and in particular a second crowded area within the very heart of Ripper territory. This was the area of Brick Lane and Sclater streets, where the old Great Eastern Railway nearby added its own atmosphere to the mean streets.

Booth spoke of streets blocked with people coming to buy and sell pigeons, canaries, rabbits, fowls, parrots, or guinea-pigs. Through this crowd, he said, the seller of shell fish pushed his barrow, while on the outskirts were

A Street seller of birds' nests

Petticoat Lane peddlers

moveable shooting galleries, and patent Aunt Sallies, while some men standing on a dog-cart "will dispose of racing tips in sealed envelopes to the East End sportsman."

He went on to say that Brick Lane "should rightly be seen Saturday night, though it is in almost all its length a gay and crowded scene every evening of the week, unless persistent rain drives both buyers and sellers to seek shelter."

Booth spoke of the flaring lights, the piles of cheap goods, and the urgent shout of the sellers which were often falling on deaf ears, a condition which he described as accepted on both sides as necessary, though entirely useless.

In describing the area in which Jack the Ripper actually disposed of three of his victims, Booth wrote: "Lying between

A typical Whitechapel street in the 1880's

Middlesex Street (Petticoat Lane) and Brick Lane are to be found most of the common lodging-houses, and in the immediate neighbourhood, lower still in reputation, there are streets of 'furnished' houses, and houses where stairways and corners are occupied nightly by those without any other shelter. So lurid and intense is the light which has lately been thrown on these quarters, that grey tones of the ordinary picture becomes invisible."

Reports

It was estimated by Booth, who used School Board visitors books as one source of assessment, that 76,000 people lived in Whitechapel in the 1800s and 909,000 in the whole East End. Delving into the mass of reports on the varying degrees of Class structure in this 'city within a city' the following is of great interest:

"The lowest class, which consists of some occasional labourers, street sellers, loafers, criminals, and semi-criminals, I put at 1¼ per cent of the population, but this is no more than a very rough estimate.... those I have attempted to count consist mostly of casual labourers of low character, and their families, together with those in a similar way of life who pick up a living without labour of any kind. Their life is the life of savages, with vicissitudes of extreme hardship and occasional

excess. Their food is of the coarsest description, and their only luxury is drink. It is not easy to say how they live; the living is picked up, and what is got is frequently shared; when they cannot find 3d for their night's lodgings, unless favourably known to the deputy, they are turned out at night into the streets, to return to the common kitchen in the morning.

Beggars

From these come the battered figures who slouch through the streets, and play the beggar on the bully, or help to foul the record of the unemployed; these are the worse class of corner men who hang round the doors of public-houses, the young men who spring forward on any chance to earn a copper, the ready materials for disorder when occasion serves. They render no useful service, they create no wealth: more often they destroy it.

Degrade

They degrade whatever they touch, and as individuals are perhaps incapable of improvement; they may be to some extent a necessary evil in every large city, but their numbers will be affected by the economical condition of the classes above them, and the discretion of 'the charitable world'; their way of life by the pressure of police supervision."

Lingering on Booth's narratives may appear to be a million miles away from Jack the Ripper and the mayhem he

caused to East End, but not only does Booth provide us with an exhaustive and vivid picture of the general appearance of Whitechapel and Spitalfields with their miscreants and unfortunate starving, but he also draws the net closer still to the very heart of the district from which Jack the Ripper chose his victims. Indeed under a heading *PROSTITUTION IN WHITECHAPEL*, Booth almost selects the very type of person that the Ripper chose to kill with apparent ease. "....many of the women are from a distance and come and go a good deal. After being herself absent for a few weeks the mission woman was struck by the number of new faces. Not a little 'poncing' is done. The bully follows closely on the heels of the pair, and asks what the stranger is doing in his room - a row, with robbery, follows, and the stranger is kicked out; or, the man having parted with some money in advance, finds himself 'bilked' and left alone and is hustled out by the neighbours. Those who enter rarely leave with money or valuables upon them...."

The first part of the above statement could justifiably fit exactly the particular pattern of life thrust upon the victims of Jack the Ripper, but, and this is hard to imagine, the East End prostitute with a 'ponce' was a great deal higher in the social scale than the Ripper victims with the possible exception of Mary Jane Kelly, whose 'boyfriend' Joseph Barnett, having lived with Kelly for some time, was possibly her 'ponce' until they parted company. But for this exception, the rest of Jack the Ripper's victims fitted best to Booth's description of a former prostitute, still living in a brothel, whom he saw feeding a cat. He described her as "in appearance she was a frowsy, debauched, drunken-looking creature."

A contemporary sketch of Joseph Barnett

Sleeping rough in Whitechapel was a part of life

The influence of the vast East End had a peculiar effect to many famous men, including American writer Jack London, who termed the residents and characters of the area as *The People of the Abyss,* an apt description.

"The City of Dreadful Monotony" and "The City of Degradation" London called the district. He also stated: "No more dreary spectacle can be found on this earth than the whole of the 'awful East', with its Whitechapel, Hoxton, Spitalfields, Bethnal Green, and Wapping to the East India Dock. The colour of life is grey and drab.

Ambrosia

He went on to describe bath tubs as a thing "totally unknown, as mythical as the ambrosia of the gods," and commented generally on the helplessness, hopelessness, and

Jack London in the guise of an East End down and out

Fighting for space in a typical Whitechapel 'penny gaff'

POLICE THE ILLUSTRATED NEWS
LAW COURTS AND WEEKLY RECORD

No. 1,284. SATURDAY, SEPTEMBER 22, 1888. Price One Penny.

"IS HE THE WHITECHAPEL MURDERER?"

READY FOR THE WHITECHAPEL FIEND. WOMEN SECRETLY ARMED.

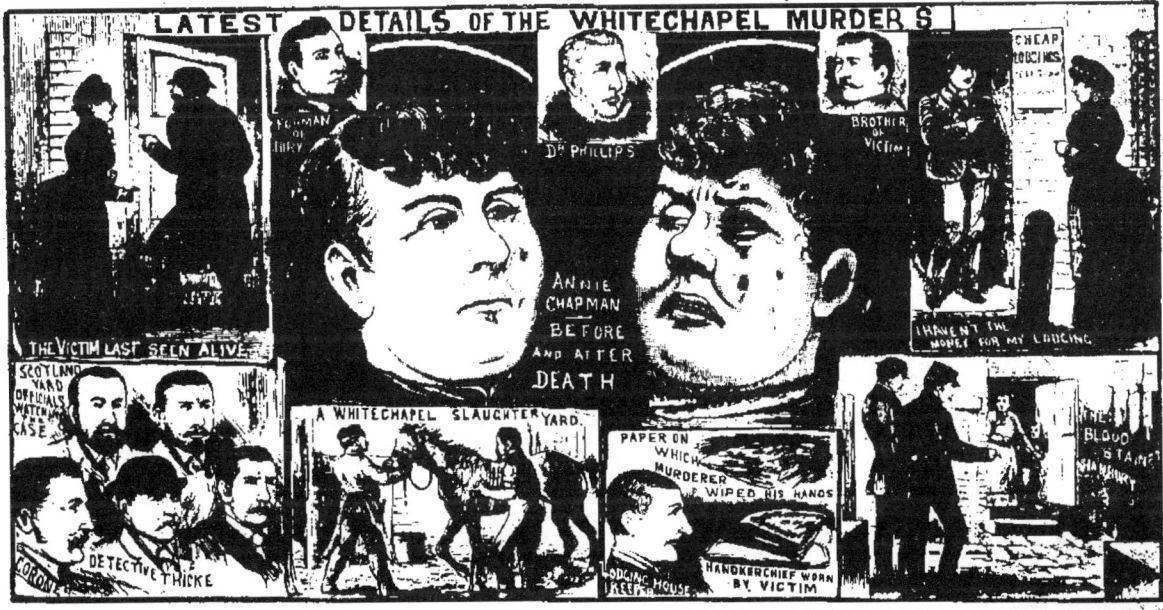

LATEST DETAILS OF THE WHITECHAPEL MURDERS

ANNIE CHAPMAN BEFORE AND AFTER DEATH

THE FIFTH VICTIM OF THE WHITECHAPEL FIEND.

FINDING THE MUTILATED BODY IN MITRE SQARE

dirtiness of everything.

"The people themselves are dirty, while any attempt of cleanliness becomes howling farce, when it is not pitiful and tragic. Strange vagrant odours come drifting along the greasy wind, and the rain, when it falls, is more like grease than water from heaven. The very cobblestones are scummed with grease."

As an American, Jack London had a neutral eye and could therefore depict

23

the East End as it was, and not as politicians would have liked the outside world to picture the chief city of the British Empire. And, like Booth, Jack London was truly appalled at what he saw and heard.

Mortality

"The high mortality of the people who live in the ghetto plays a terrible part. The average age of death among the people of the West End is fifty-five years; the average age of death among the people of the East End is thirty years," he wrote. He continued by pointing out that in the West End eighteen per cent of the children died before reaching five years of age, while in the 'abyss' *fifty-five per cent* (my italics) of the children died before five years of age.

This high mortality rate in the East End is hardly surprising when we look at the findings of the Reverend W.N. Davies, Rector of Spitalfields, who took a census of some of the alleyways in his parish and found some astonishing facts. In one alley, for example, where stood ten houses comprising of fifty one rooms, he found 254 people

Astonishing

He also found that in only six instances did two people occupy one room, while in others the numbers ranged from three to nine people in each room. Even more astonishing was his count of forty-five people living in one house of only eight rooms.

Policemen worked in pairs in the 'Abyss'

A street seller of sheet music

something like humans and more like beasts, and to complete the picture, brass-buttoned keepers kept order among them when they snarled too fiercely.

Keepers

"I was glad the keepers were there, for I did not have on my 'seafaring' clothes, and I was what is called a 'mark' for the creatures of prey that prowled up and down. At times, between keepers, these males looked at me, sharply, hungrily, gutter-wolves that they were, and I was afraid of their hands, of their naked hands, as one may be afraid of the paws of a gorilla. Their bodies were small, ill-shaped and squat. There were no swelling muscles, no abundant thews and wide-spreading shoulders. They exhibited, rather, an elemental economy of nature, such as the cave-men must have exhibited. But there was strength in those meagre bodies, the ferocious,

But Jack London's descriptions of this district are highly potent, and he wrote: "Last night I walked along Commercial Street from Spitalfields to Whitechapel, and still continuing south, down Leman Street to the docks. And as I walked I smiled at the East End papers, which, filled with civic pride, boastfully proclaim that there is nothing the matter with the East End as a living place for men and women.

"It is rather hard to tell a tithe of what I saw. Much of it is untellable. But in a general way I may say that I saw a nightmare, a fearful slime that quickened the pavement with life, a mess of unmentionable obscenity that put into eclipse the 'nightly horror' of Piccadilly and the Strand. It was a menagerie of garmented bipeds that looked

A flower seller

The Nemesis of Neglect,
a contemporary cartoon of police impotence

Dorset Street, Spitalfields, once the most dangerous
street in London

Buying and selling in the East End
in the heart of Ripper territory

Actor Laird Cregar is pictured as Jack the Ripper in the 1944 film *The Lodger*, a remake of the more famous Hitchcock film of the same name.

A contemporary sketch of the Whitechapel killer

primeval strength to clutch and gripe and tear and rend.

"When they spring upon their human prey they are known even to bend the victim backward and double its body till the back is broken. They possess neither conscience or sentiment, and they will kill for half-sovereign, without fear or favour, if they are given but half a chance. They are a new species, a breed of city savages. The streets and houses, alleys and courts, are their hunting ground. As valley and mountain are to the natural savage, street and building are valley and mountain to them. The slum is their jungle, and they live and prey in the jungle....

"But they were not the only beasts that ranged the menagerie. They were only here and there, lurking in dark courts

The Nemesis of Neglect
A contemporary sketch of the 1888 Ripper scare

and passing like grey shadows along the walls; but the women from whose rotten loins they spring were everywhere. They whined insolently, and in maudlin tones begged me for pennies, and worse. They held carouse in every boozing ken, slatternly, unkempt, bleary-eyed, and towsled, leering and gibbering, overspilling with foulness and corruption, and, gone in debauch, sprawling across benches and bars, unspeakably repulsive, fearful to look upon."

The writings of London and Booth are shocking for their intimate look at Whitechapel and Spitalfields, but, like it or not, these were the districts which were frequented by the victims of Jack the Ripper and could, perhaps, go some way to explaining why the killer chose his victims from the dregs of late Victorian society.

The search goes on

I mentioned earlier that I believed Jack the Ripper was a part of the dreadful Whitechapel and Spitalfields community and this assumption must be borne in mind when we consider the intimacy with which he obviously knew the narrow streets and alleyways. There are a number of logical points to bear in mind, namely that he was able to walk the streets without fear (witness the fear of Jack London); he was able to traverse the streets which others found alarmingly similar to a maze (therefore showing local knowledge); he was able to approach several of his victims (with the possible exception of Nichols) without rousing their suspicion that he was to be feared. The latter point is very important if we remember that after the killings of Nichols and Chapman the public were almost at panic stations. To approach 'street wise' prostitutes in mid-Ripper scare suggests strongly that he was someone with whom victims could identify (perhaps in more ways than one?) and therefore gain their confidence easily and quickly.

Some writers have suggested this could easily be a local policeman, but it is very doubtful since prostitutes of the East End (as elsewhere) would certainly go out of their way to avoid contact with the

Commercial Street, Spitalfields, in the very heart of Ripper territory. The Ten Bells pub is on the right with Dorset Street and the Britannia pub on the left

law. Evidence of the general hatred or dislike for the police is shown clearly in Robin Odell's assessment of the need for many officers to patrol the streets in pairs - and especially Dorset Street, variably described as 'The do as you please' and 'The most dangerous street in London'.

Suspicious

Jack the Ripper, therefore, *had* to be someone with whom the victims showed no fear or even remotely suspicious. Who fitted into this category bearing in mind also the time of night when the killings took place? A Doctor? Possibly, but unlikely since once again local prostitutes were hardly likely to have any

close contact with them on two counts: The first being simply financial. In those far off days it cost money to see an M.D., and the victims could not have afforded to pay for a doctor even if they wanted to (they would have preferred to spend such money on drink and lodgings in that order); secondly there is the question of a doctor's appearance. He would have been undoubtedly well dressed even in the middle of the night if he was making a call. This would have deterred the prostitute who would have been suspicious of such a well dressed 'gent'.

Slaughterman

A common slaughterman? Possibly, but again unlikely since rumours soon ran wild in the area that police were looking for a slaughterman suspect, and even the hardest character usually avoided passing the doors of slaughterhouse with its horrible mixture of smells and blood. A slaughterman, by the very nature of his work, would have had blood stained on their clothing and the stench of death upon him. This, I believe, would have made a casual, friendly approach almost out of the question.

Bucks Row, scene of Mary Nichols murder

Midwife

A Midwife? Hardly more likely than the M.D., since it was extremely common at that time for children to be delivered by grand-mothers or other friends and relatives. We must remember that these Londoners were extremely tough and adaptable even if they were on or below the poverty line. They would not bring in outside help unless it was absolutely necessary.

With possibly one or two exceptions, this leaves us with the likeliest choice of all - a Clergyman. The type of clergyman does not really matter, eg Church of England or Roman Catholic. The important point to consider is that if he was wearing clerical garb complete with 'dog-collar' he would find approaching even the lowliest prostitute relatively easy.

approaching churchman. Even prostitutes of Victorian England would have held a lot of respect for a 'man of the cloth' even if the prostitutes were not noted for churchgoing.

I mentioned above that Mary Ann Nichols was the possible exception with

Durward Street (late Bucks Row) in the 1920s

Prostitute

The prostitute would have nothing to fear (or so they would presume) from an

the approach I have outlined, and I make this statement only because it is a recorded fact that Nichols was the worse for drink on the night she was murdered. Evidence of Nichols' inebriation was given by the last woman to see her alive, another prostitute called Emily Holland who met the doomed Nichols at 2.30 A.M., on the morning of August 31, 1888. According to Mrs Holland, Mary Ann Nichols had confided that she had been turned out of her lodgings in Thrawl Street because she did not have fourpence for a bed. After exchanging a few words, including the information that she was going to walk along Whitechapel Road in the hope of getting the money, Nichols staggered on her way. That was approximately an hour or so before her body was found half a mile away in Bucks Row.

Drunk

Obviously a woman of desperate needs, slightly drunk, would not look too closely at an approaching male. In fact she would probably be happy to be approached, thinking this was a likely 'client' from whom she could extract the fourpence she so badly needed.

Puzzling

What is still puzzling investigators today as it certainly was in 1888, is *why* was Nichols attacked that fateful night? *Why* did the man soon to go into history books as Jack the Ripper choose to start his desperate campaign against Whitechapel 'unfortunates' (as prostitutes were known)? Obviously it is a mystery which will last forever, for no suitable motive has been put forward. In his book *Jack the Ripper: The Final Solution*, the late Stephen Knight gave the opinion that Nichols and her contemporaries were all killed as part of a conspiracy which involved the British Royal Family. While not denying that

thereabouts (the approximate time Nichols was killed) is ludicrous. For a start, Nichols herself had no idea where she was going so why on earth should a group of conspiratorial assassins? Are we seriously expected to believe that Nichols was followed all night from 'boozing ken' to Bucks Row?

Motive

But whatever the motive behind the attack on poor 'Polly' Nichols, there is no doubt that her killing seemed to have sparked off something within the brain of her still anonymous killer; a spark which ultimately saw the savage deaths of four more prostitutes.

Examining behind the facade of the general story relating to Jack the Ripper it is astonishing how similar his attacks were in their locations. It has always been plainly stated that *all* the killings took place in the street (with the exception of Mary Jane Kelly who was butchered in her tiny hovel in Millers Court), but this is not necessarily true.

If we look again at the locations we will note that all the murders took place near or in an enclosed yard or space. When Nichols was found her body was lying parallel to the double gates of a stable *yard;* Annie Chapman, murdered a week later, was found in the back *yard* of 29 Hanbury Street; Elizabeth Stride's body was discovered in Dutfield's *Yard* off Berner Street; the corpse of Catherine Eddowes was discovered in Mitre *Square.*

Coincidental

The similarity is clear enough to make the investigator wonder whether this was coincidental or not. My own thoughts are inclined to believe that it was not coincidental. Such places provided Jack the Ripper with perfect cover to allow him, if necessary, to wait for considerable periods of time in order to attack his selected victims. Just why he picked the victims he did, can, however, be a matter of pure speculation.

The Jack the Ripper case presents the serious investigator with more 'mysteries within a mystery' than any other case in the annals of crime. Not only are investigators faced with the inevitable questions Who? and Why? but are equally perplexed with a series of strange happenings, events and contradictions which only makes the 'maze' seem never ending. Let us look at some of these complexities.

In the Nichols case a Mrs Emma Green who lived at New Cottage in Bucks Row claims that despite being a light sleeper she heard nothing until police knocked on her door at 4am on August 31. She told the inquest jury: "I don't remember waking up until I heard a knock at the front door about four in the morning. I opened the window and saw three or four constables and two or three other men. I saw the body lying on the floor but it was too dark to see much. I heard nothing unusual during the night...I am a light sleeper and if there had been a scream I'm sure I would have heard it."

Walter Purkiss, manager of Essex Wharf which stood almost opposite the murder site, told the inquest: "I woke up from time to time during the night and I was awake between one and two. I did not hear anything until I was called up

Spitalfields Market pictured in 1938 shortly after redevelopment saw the disappearance of Dorset Street which stood on the extreme left of the picture

by the police at four o' clock. My wife was awake most of the night. Neither of us heard a sound during the night and it was unusually quiet."

Now compare these statements with the evidence of PC 97 Neil of J Division, who told the jury: "I was proceeding down Bucks Row, Whitechapel, going

Flower and Dean Street in Spitalfields pictured in 1928, just 40 years after the Ripper killings and little changed. This scene no longer exists, and the street has been renamed Lolesworth Close!

towards Brady Street...when I noticed a figure lying in the street. It was dark at the time though there was a street lamp shining at the end of the row. I went across and found the deceased lying outside a gateway, head towards the east...I examined the body by the aid of my lamp and noticed blood oozing from a wound in the throat...I heard a constable passing Brady Street (about 50 yards away) so I called him. I said 'Run for Doctor Llewellyn'."

This is confusing. If PC Neil "heard" a fellow constable passing Brady Street and then shouted him to assist, then surely his voice must have been loud enough to be heard in New Cottage and Essex Wharf respectively if it was loud enough to be heard 50 yards away?

Notoriety

It would suggest that the witnesses Green and Purkiss were not such light sleepers as they would suggest, or were merely seeking notoriety, and therefore their statements can be ruled as unreliable. Alternatively, perhaps PC Neil's statement was also exaggerated which makes the evidence at the inquest even more unreliable and confusing.

And it is with such unreliable evidence that Jack the Ripper was not only lucky but relatively safe when it came to carrying out his dark deeds.

Example

We will take as another example a claim made, after the murder of 'Dark Annie' Chapman in Hanbury Street, by John Davis, a porter at nearby Spitalfields Market. He is alleged to have stated that he heard a clock strike six, climbed out of bed and made himself some tea before going into the back yard at 29 Hanbury Street where he found the mutilated remains of Chapman. By 6.10am Inspector Chandler of Commercial Street police station had been informed of the murder. That is a lot to happen in *10* minutes! How is it possible for someone to climb out of bed, make tea, visit the yard, discover a dead body, apparently suffer no shock (or at least insufficient to detain him) and notify the local police all in the space of those few minutes? Somewhere along the line there is something wrong!

A sketch of Mary Ann Nichols in the mortuary from a magazine of the period

There was something wrong too in the opinion of local Divisional Surgeon, Dr George Bagster Phillips who believed Annie Chapman had been dead for at least two hours when he examined her body at 6.30 A.M., on the morning of September 8. He did concede, however, that this opinion could have been influenced by the coldness of the morning, but it was a sad statement from a man who had practiced medicine for 20 years.

Even allowing for some error in his assessment of the time of death it was later shown that his judgement was out by at least 90 minutes if we are to believe a claim by a Mrs Long who told police that she had been walking along Hanbury Street in the direction of Spitalfields Market at 5.30 A.M., when she saw Chapman talking to a man just

Below: The rear yard of 29 Hanbury Street where Annie Chapman was found dead

The front of 29 Hanbury Street, Spitalfields. Annie Chapman met her fate when she accompanied Jack the Ripper through the doorway pictured closed in the centre

outside number 29 Hanbury Street.

The Berner Street killing of Elizabeth Stride, also known as 'Long Liz', also presents some conflicting statements and only adds to the general confusion of that which surrounds all the murders of Jack the Ripper.

Drizzle

In his book *Autumn of Terror* published in 1965, author Tom Cullen noted that Louis Diemschutz, the man who discovered Stride's body in Dutfield's Yard in Berner Street at 1 A.M., on the morning of September 1, 1888, had spent the previous evening trying to sell his cheap wares, namely jewellery, outside the Crystal Palace, Sydenham, which was his usual hawking pitch. He decided to leave this pitch, however, at 11.30 P.M., or a little after as it had, according to Cullen, begun to drizzle. If this was the case, *why was the ground dry* beneath the body of Elizabeth Stride when she was discovered 90 minutes later? This is a point mentioned by Robin Odell in his book *Jack the Ripper In Fact And Fiction,* but there has been no logical and convincing answer from anyone for the past century. According to medical experts at the time, Stride had only been dead a few minutes when she was found by Diemschutz, a point borne out by the hawker's claim that the woman's blood was still pouring from her cut throat when he discovered her.

Confusing

There is yet another confusing aspect of the Elizabeth Stride killing when we consider statements made by people who should have made vitally

The outside of 29 Hanbury Street, pictured in 1965, and looking unchanged from the 1880s

Elizabeth Stride

kitchen door of the club. A little - that nearest to her on the ground - was slightly congealed." This seems a remarkably quick time for blood to congeal, especially allowing for the cold, damp night.

Then there is further confusion caused by the evidence of Dr Frederick Blackwell, one of three doctors who examined the corpse. Dr Blackwell said: "The blood was running down the gutter into the drain in the opposite direction from the feet.....In my opinion she had been dead for twenty minutes to half an hour when I arrived. *The clothes were not wet with rain* (my italics)." Now compare this with a claim made by Tom Cullen in *Autumn of Terror* who wrote: "Her head was resting almost in line with the carriageway. *Her clothes were wet,* but when they moved the body the police noticed that the ground beneath it was quite dry." Which is correct?

important witnesses. The first is a statement made in evidence by Police Constable Henry Lamb. He claimed...."Some of the blood was in a liquid state and had run towards the

Discovering the body of Elizabeth 'Long Liz' Stride

A contemporary sketch of women secretly arming themselves

Then there is the even more confusing statement made by a Mrs Mortimer who lived at 36 Berner Street, four doors from Dutfield's Yard. According to a report which appeared in the *Manchester Guardian* and other newspapers, she said: "I was standing at the door of my house nearly the whole time between half-past twelve and one o' clock this morning, and did not notice anything unusual. I had just gone indoors and was preparing to go to bed when I heard a commotion outside, and immediately ran out, thinking that there was a row at the Socialists' Club close by. I went to see what was the matter, and was informed that another murder had been committed in the yard adjoining the clubhouse. On going inside I saw the body of a woman lying huddled up just within the gates, with her throat cut. A man touched her face, and said it was quite warm, so that the deed must have been done while I was standing at the

Another sketch of finding Elizabeth Stride's body

door of my house. There was certainly no noise made, and I did not observe anyone enter the gates. It was just after one o' clock when I went out, and the only man whom I had seen pass through the street previously was a young man *carrying a black shiny bag,* (my italics) who walked very fast down the street from the Commercial Road. He looked up at the club, and then went round the corner by the Board school..."

Contradicts

This statement contradicts a claim made by a Russian named Morris Eagle who said he had left the club at midnight to take his sweetheart home before

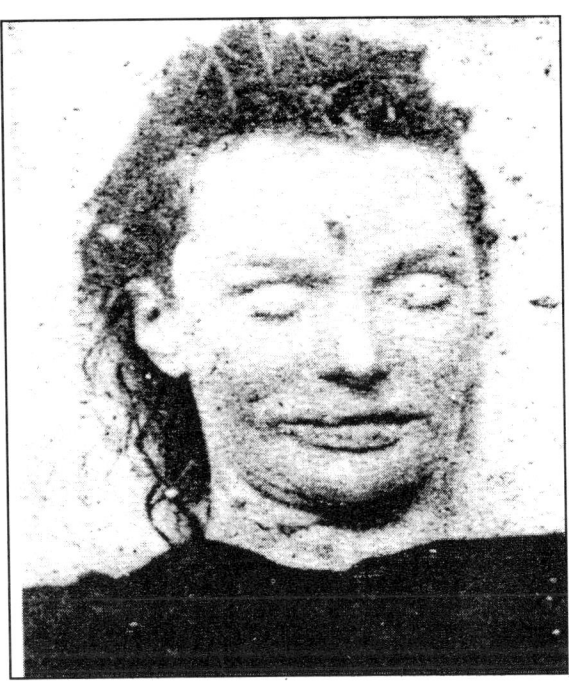

Elizabeth Stride in the morgue

Berner Street, Whitechapel. Stride was murdered in Dutfield's Yard, which stood through the gates shown in the centre of the picture

returning to the premises at approximately 12.40 am. To enter the yard where Stride's body was found would have made it necessary to have passed within the view of Mrs Mortimer, yet she claimed she saw no one except the stranger with that mysterious shiny black bag!

Again I would be inclined to take a lot of what Mrs Mortimer said as exaggeration. Jack the Ripper was hardly likely to carry such a bag after the scare which had swept through the district after the previous killings when shiny black bags - the Gladstone bag - suddenly became a symbol of the killer.

Macabre

That is not to say that people with a macabre desire for notoriety did not stalk the streets of the East End at the height of the Ripper scare. There is another report in the *Manchester Guardian* of Tuesday, October 2, 1888, which tells the tale of a young man called Albert Baebert, of Newnham Street, Whitechapel, who alleged that while he was in the Three Tuns Hotel on the night of the murders of Elizabeth Stride and Catherine Eddowes, a man spoke to him in detail, trying to obtain detailed information on the regular whereabouts of prostitutes.

Baebert said "On Saturday night, at about seven minutes to twelve, I entered the Three Tuns Hotel, Aldgate. While in there an elderly woman, very shabbily dressed, came in and asked

me to buy some matches. I refused, and she went out. A man who had been standing by me remarked that those persons were a nuisance, to which I responded 'Yes.' He then asked me how old some of the women were who were in the habit of soliciting outside...He asked me if I could tell him where they usually went with men, and I replied that I had heard that some went to places in Oxford Street, Whitechapel, and others to Bishopsgate Street. He then asked whether I thought they would go with him down Northumberland Alley, a dark and lonely court in Fenchurch Street.... He was a dark man, about 38 years of age,

height about 5ft. 6in. or 7in. He wore a black felt hat, dark clothes (morning coat, black tie, *and carried a black, shiny bag* (my italics)."

This type of description appeared again in the newspapers of the period and it soon became evident that anyone seen with such a black shiny bag was putting his life in peril. East End mobs actively pursued strangers through the streets of Whitechapel and Spitalfields - and often further afield - if they held the slightest suspicion that they were on the trail of Jack the Ripper.

But Jack the Ripper was far smarter than anyone gave him credit for. Police, vigilante committees, newspaper reporters, amateur detectives - they were all confident that they would track the killer down - but, of course, they never did!

The list of suspects grew even longer and dozens of people each day were taken into custody for questioning, all without success. The number of strange contradictions in the case increased with each murder and only made the task of the police more difficult. Of course it is always as well to remember that we are taking about a police force which was not particularly professional, at least not within its Detective Department, and it was headed by two of the most unsuitable characters for police work. First there was the Chief Commissioner, General Sir Charles Warren, an overbearing military man with absolutely no experience of police work and the 'softly-softly' approach that the policemen needed to function

Whitechapel at the turn of the century

**Sir Charles Warren
Scotland Yard Commissioner**

equately. He thought the Metropolitan Police should be run on military line which was a grave mistake because it stifled initiative.

Then there was the new Assistant Commissioner Robert Anderson, an Irish lawyer who, like his boss, had no experience of police work. He showed all the delicacy of a bull in a china shop by going to Europe for a month's rest only a week after his appointment, despite the fact that Nichols had been murdered the day before he joined the Metropolitan Police, and Chapman only a matter of hours before he left the country for Switzerland! With such insensitivity it is hardly surprising that the morale of the police force was at a low ebb during the Ripper investigations.

Sir Robert Anderson

The extent of Warren's incompetence, or concern, (depending on your point of view) was shown clearly after the murder of Catherine Eddowes in Mitre Square. A piece of Eddowes' apron had been cut off by Jack the Ripper and was found discarded next to a public tap in Goulston Street, Whitechapel. Nearby a chalked message was also discovered allegedly making disparaging remarks about the Jewish population of Whitechapel. Warren had the message rubbed out. There has been a lot of comment throughout the years on this point but space does not permit another inquiry here. Instead, let us look at the significance of the piece of apron. In my view this find was highly significant for I believe it told the police not merely that Jack the Ripper was heading in North Easterly direction but in fact it directed them towards the Ripper's hiding place!

Puzzled

It has always puzzled investigators how Jack the Ripper managed to kill so easily then escape the scenes without apparent trace. There have been many questions asked about the killer's bloodstained appearance as he travelled the streets in full view of the population. It has always been strongly suggested that Jack the Ripper *must* have been bloodstained. Even eminent physicians at the time of the murders took this view. But I am of the opinion that they were wrong. Robin Odell gave a logical explanation for his belief that the Ripper was not bloodstained when he explained in *Jack the Ripper in Fact and Fiction* that a *shochet* a Jewish ritual slaughterman, would have eliminated this possibility by kicking the victim away at the moment of death. But there is another possible explanation.

All the alleged sightings of Jack the Ripper depict him carrying a bag or a parcel. Shortly before Mary Jane Kelly was slaughtered it was claimed by a man called George Hutchinson that Kelly had been approached by a man who had been standing at the corner of Thrawl Street and that she went with him to her lodgings in nearby Miller's Court. According to Hutchinson the man with Kelly "carried a small parcel in his hand."

Speculated

Many writers, and no doubt policemen, have speculated that within these bags and parcels was the knives used by Jack the Ripper. Hardly a logical conclusion in view of the panic stricken East End. If Jack the Ripper carried a knife or knives it is more than likely that

he secreted them on his person. So what was in the parcel carried by the man with Kelly?

Cassock

I believe that parcel (and the earlier shiny bags if they belonged to the Ripper) contained nothing more innocent looking than a religious *Cassock!* This, I believe, was the reason Jack the Ripper was able to get away so easily. He wasn't *obviously* covered with blood at all. I am of the opinion that after each murder (with the possible exception of Elizabeth Stride) he donned this garment over his 'work clothes' which he wore for the killings. A cassock would be ideal for this purpose on two counts.One: a cassock being a

Whitechapel High Street in the 1880s

Mitre Square, scene of the murder of Catherine Eddowes

long close fitting tunic, normally black, and buttoning to the neck as well as reaching to the ankles would have provided *in seconds* an instant disguise for any bloodstained clothing. This would have made Jack the Ripper immediately invisible from suspicion. Two: as I mentioned earlier a man 'of the cloth' was a familiar sight in Whitechapel and Spitalfields and would have attracted no suspicion whatsoever. Indeed a Minster could have gone anywhere at any time.

Different

So now we look at the Jack the Ripper killings in a slightly different way. We are no longer looking for a maniac prowling the streets with a dripping knife in his hand; we are no longer looking for a slaughterman with his leather apron; we are no longer looking for a 'toff' with his well-dressed appearance. In fact we are looking for a religious minister who (1) knew the district intimately, (2) who was able to approach the victims without suspicion, (3) who was able to calmly walk through the streets without attracting attention to himself.

Exception

The exception of Elizabeth Stride is answered by the obvious lack of time Jack the Ripper had to don this garment in Dutfield's Yard due to the unexpected interruption of Louis Diemschutz. This

Two views of Mitre Square as it looks today after extensive alterations

does not, however, prevent the killer from escaping easily because in this case he would hardly be likely to be bloodstained in the first place since he had not had time to mutilate Stride's body.

Forty minutes later when he killed and savagely slashed Catherine Eddowes in Mitre Square his fury knew no bounds. Obviously frustrated in his urge to kill and mutilate he made up for his lack of evisceration to Stride by excelling himself in the cutting

Two 19th century views of Christ Church, Spitalfields

of Eddowes. It is noteworthy that it was after the murder of Eddowes that the killer found it necessary to cut a piece of his victim's apron off in order to clean himself up in Goulston Street. Having satiated his evil he headed to Whitechapel on his way to sanctuary when he realised his hands were bloodstained. This would have been understandable when it is realised the speed and conditions under which he killed in Mitre Square.

Black

The corner of the square where he murdered Eddowes was almost pitch black and he would have been working almost by touch alone. Compare the darkness of Mitre Square with Bucks Row (a street lamp nearby); Hanbury Street (dawn was rising); Berner Street (some light from the International Socialists Club) and Miller's Court (where a candle and a fierce fire in the grate was available).

This, I believe, is a logical explanation for the use of the discarded apron. He would have realised that by working in the dark a certain amount of blood was inevitable and would require cleaning. He obviously knew of the public tap and sink in Goulston Street for it is certain he headed directly there.

Cunning

All this activity by Jack the Ripper shows more than mere animal cunning. It is yet another example of his intimate knowledge of the district. It is also, in my opinion, a clue to how the killer disappeared so easily after each murder, and therefore a clue to his possible identify This may seem a rash statement to make and I could be accused on jumping on the 'Identify the Ripper' bandwagon, but I hope logic and not emotion will overcome any such suggestion. We can examine each

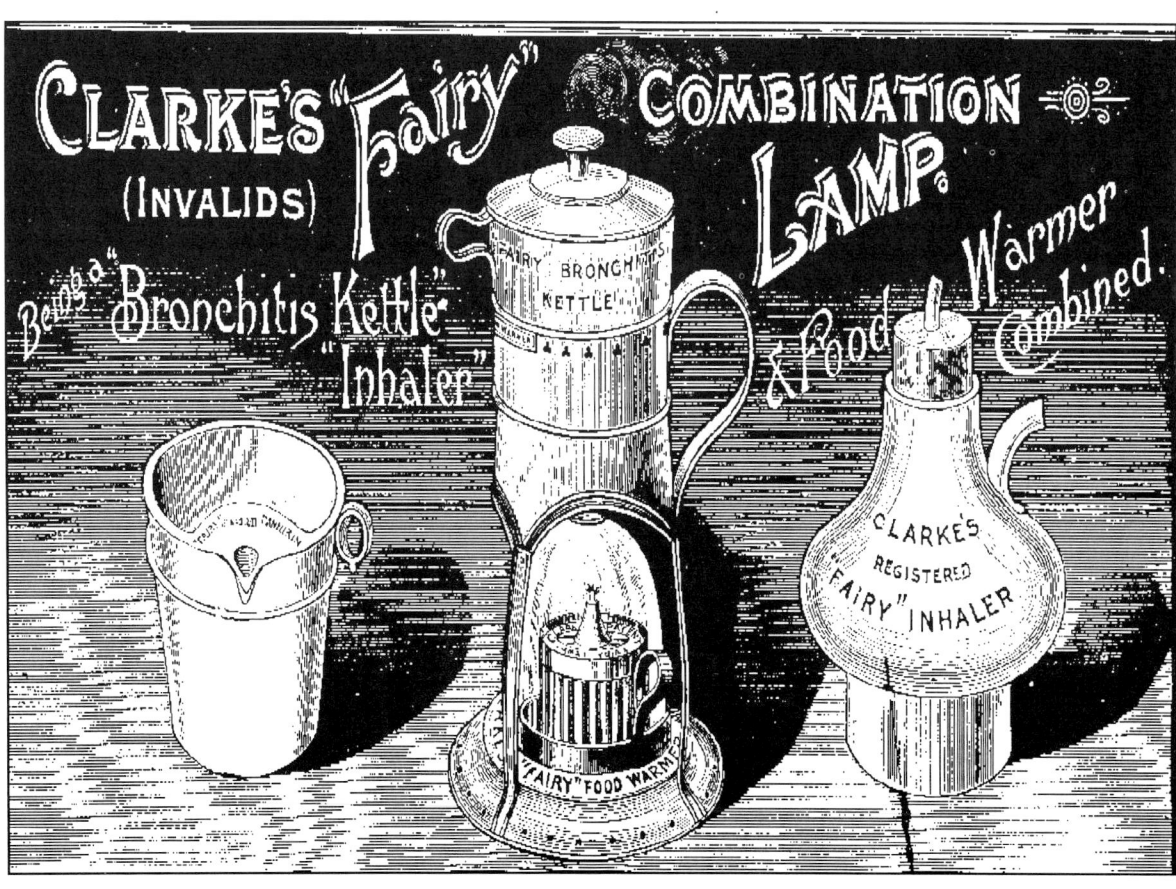

Miller's Court, scene of Mary Kelly's murder, was down this passageway in the centre of Dorset Street

murder again briefly and we see if we can find an 'escape route' for Jack.

Escaped

Bearing in mind my belief that Jack the Ripper was a Minster who cleverly disguised himself with a Cassock after each killing it must be asked in the first place how he escaped from Bucks Row? If he had made for Brady Street after killing Nichols he would have probably encountered Police Constable Haine (or Thaine) whose beat that was. If he had headed for Hanbury Street he would have encountered Police Constable Neil. Besides these officers he would probably have bumped into other patrolling policemen as well as two men on their way to work at the nearby Spitalfields Market, William Cross and John Paul. This is a point made by author Donald McCormick in his book *The Identity of Jack the Ripper.* McCormick wrote "What was even more remarkable was that five men - PCs Haine, Nizen and Neil, Cross and Paul - all approaching Bucks Row from different directions....saw not a single person."

Remarkable

It was indeed remarkable that Jack the Ripper could have bypassed all these people. *It is my belief that he did not leave Bucks Row at all!* Where then did the killer go? By examining a street

Map of Whitechapel

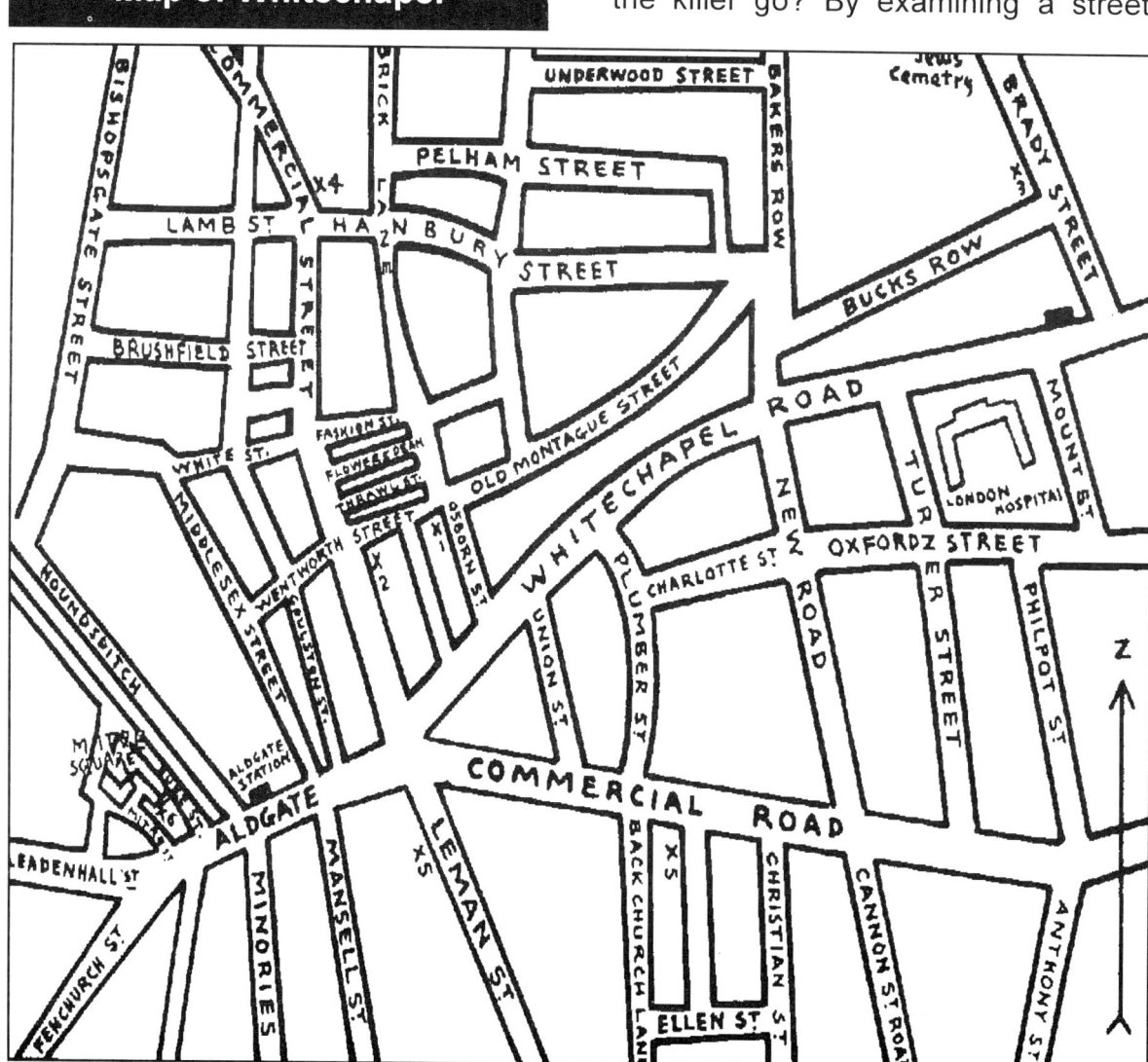

directory for Bucks Row it will be noticed that within a few yards of where Nicholls was killed there existed a *Clergy House.* It is my belief that Jack the Ripper in his clerical garb sought refuse in this house under the pretext of finding the body across the street. He could have cheerfully made up a fabricated tale of having bloodstains on his hands due to examining a poor 'unfortunate woman'.

Welcomed

Fellow ministers of the church would have accepted such a tale without much trouble and would have welcomed him in their midst. And there is further circumstantial evidence to back up this claim.

According to William Stewart, author of *Jack the Ripper: A New Theory,* a local policeman, Inspector Spratley, returned to Bucks Row to examine the crime scene and found "there were traces of blood in the interstices of the pavement where the woman's head had laid."

He carefully examined the whole length of the street on both sides, and some short distance away from where the body had laid *had discovered several large spots of blood.* These spots were on *the opposite side of the road* (my italics) and in the centre of the pavement, from their appearance he would say that they may possibly have

dripped from the murderer as he walked away." In other words what Stewart was describing was Inspector Spratley finding bloodstains heading in the direction of the Clergy House.

Interesting

What is also interesting is the fact that the inspector did not call at every house in Bucks Row during his investigation. Why not? Was it possibly because he would think it ungentlemanly to question the three reverend gentlemen who lived in Bucks Row Clergy House?

Quoting William Stewart again, he noted: "From the scene of the murder up to Brady Street is 160 paces and to the lower end of Bucks Row fifty paces,

Winthrop St pictured from Bucks Row in the 1960s and unchanged since 1888

which proves (from the blood stains that the murderer left by the longest way possible, unlike most murderers, who hasten from the scenes of their crimes by the shortest route possible." From Stewart's point of view it is a pity he did not realise the significance of the Clergy House.

Blood

With the murder of Annie Chapman in Hanbury Street we have the same problem of how Jack the Ripper escaped. But this too presents little problem. If he had blood on his hands

after mutilating Chapman, there was a tap in the back yard of number 29 Hanbury Street within two yards of where she was killed. And directly across the street from number 29 was the United Methodist Free Church, an easy place of sanctuary for someone in clerical garb.

Interrupted

Turning now to the 'Double Event' on September 30, 1888. We should remember that this night turned into a double killing only because Jack the Ripper was interrupted in Berner Street.

The United Methodist Free Church, Hanbury Street, in 1996

But what plans he had made for an escape in the event of his planned single murder? It is interesting to note that within two or three hundred yards of Berner Street, at the junction of Whitechapel Road and Union Street, stood St Mary Matfelon Church - another easy refuge for the killer.

Fury

His hasty departure, in a fury, from Berner Street, drove Jack the Ripper to Mitre Square (a coincidental religious name!) from where he was forced to head to Goulston Street because he had made no plans for sanctuary in that area. He was undoubtedly heading for the nearest church with which he *was* familiar. The church of St Mary's, Spital Square, a mere 100 yards further on from Goulston Street.

Safety

St Mary's Church in Spital Square was also, I believe, Jack the Ripper's place

of safety after the glut in killing Mary Jane Kelly in Dorset Street. Here he was a mere 50 yards away from the sanctuary he so desperately needed. And in the event of having to change his plans again as in the case of the 'Double Event' he had the benefit of nearby Christ Church at the corner of Fournier Street and Commercial Street, again a mere 50 yards away!

One further important point to remember is that in the 19th century *all* these churches would have been accessible twenty four hours a day. This, I think, offers a logical answer to the question of how the killer escaped the scenes of murders so easily. But what of the man himself?

Clues

There are certain clues to the possible identity of Jack the Ripper if some of the 'sightings' are to be believed. Let us return, for example, to the statement of George Hutchinson. He described the man he saw with Mary Jane Kelly as 'looking like a foreigner' and added 'I believe that he lives in the neighbourhood'.

These are more significant comments than they might first appear. It had always been the general view of the police and the press at the time that the murders, by their very bestiality, could not have been the work of an Englishman, and while this sentiment can be forgiven by an Empire loving British population there was an element of truth in what they said.

Such barbaric mutilations as those carried out by Jack the Ripper were unique in the annals of British crime, and it is in this barbarism that we must look for clues. Such ferocity in late 19th century Britain was totally unknown - indeed it was extremely rare in the rest of the world at that period - with the exception of one part of the world, Turkey.

Despots

For centuries the despots of Turkey had not only ordered millions killed by all manner of revolting methods, but even in the latter part of the Victorian era such killings were commonplace in that country. Only twelve years before the Ripper murders the world was stunned by newspaper reports from Turkey after atrocities had been reported. The British Government ordered their Constantinople Embassy to investigate the allegations and the Embassy reported that Turkish troops had committed "the most heinous crime that had stained the history of the present century."

Gladstone

Even the former British Prime Minister William Ewart Gladstone (ironically the man who gave his name to the notorious 'Ripper' bags) was sufficiently moved to write a pamphlet that the Turks were "the great anti-human specimen of humanity." The Turks, under order from Sultan Abdul Aziz, had murdered over 12,000 men, women and children and burnt 60 villages to the ground. And his successor, an even worse despot, Sultan Abdul Hamid II, ordered the merciless killing of 100,000 Armenians.

In their book *The World's Most Evil Men* authors Neil Blandford and Bruce Jones, wrote on this subject and added: "..Westerners witnessed the terror in Trebizond, where every Christian house was plundered before the owners *were ritually slaughtered, their throats cut as if they were sheep."* (my italics).

It can be seen clearly that of all the places in the world at the time of Jack the Ripper the 'ritual slaughter' and the throat cuttings so much a modus operandi of the

Now used for carpet storage, this was 24 New Street where Joseph Barnet lived after leaving Mary Kelly, shortly before she was killed by Jack the Ripper

William Ewart Gladstone, the British Prime Minister who gave his name to the notorious Gladstone bag

Whitechapel killer was carried out unhindered only in Turkey. This could be an explanation of all the reports of Jack the Ripper being 'a foreigner'.

Connection

So what are we left with? We know that we are looking for a clergyman with an intimate knowledge of Whitechapel who looked like a foreigner, probably with a Turkish connection to explain the peculiarly brutal method of murder which was so unknown in Victorian London.

Where do we begin to search for such a man? In my case I started searching the very useful Crockford's Clerical Directory for 1888, and after extensive research I found what I believe is the answer on page 403 of that directory. Listed under the name *John Moses*

Eppstein was the information I wanted.

Priest

Eppstein became a Deacon in 1858 and a Priest in 1862. He was at one time Head Missionary of the London Jewish Society, and afterwards a lecturer at the Jewish Episcopal Chapel in Palestine Place, London, and a Principal of the Wanderers Home for inquiring and believing Jews in 1887. But the interesting part of Eppstein's career shows that between 1867 and 1885 he was a Missionary at Smyrna (now Izmir), the third largest city in Turkey. He was also a Missionary at Bournabat, near Smyrna, between 1867-70 and a Missionary at Boudjah, also near Smyrna, from 1885 to 1887.

These dates are interesting in that they also offer a possible reason for the Jack the Ripper killings starting when they did. It would have taken Eppstein

Lord Salisbury, who was Prime Minister at the time of the Ripper murders

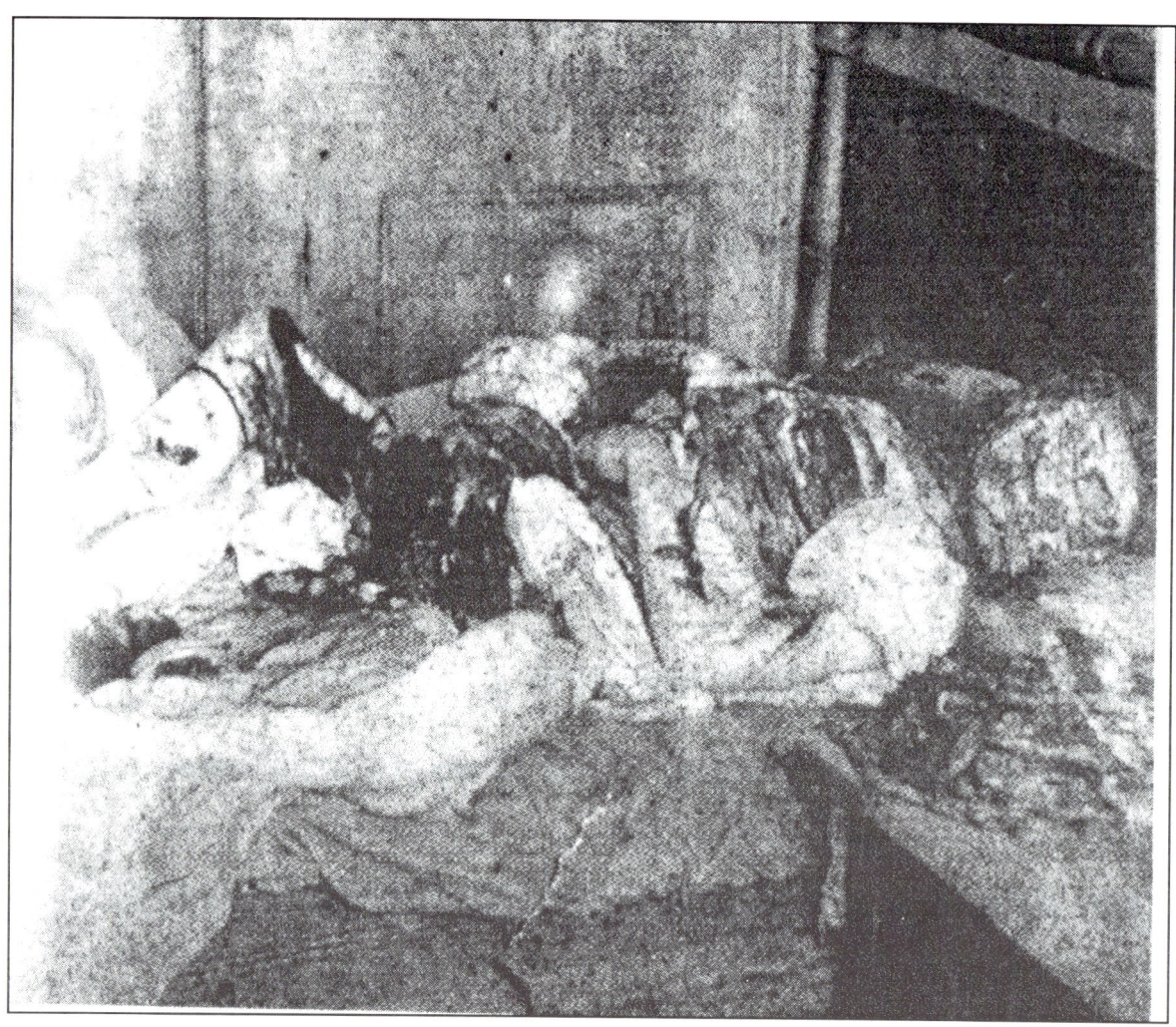

Mary Jane Kelly, the final victim of Jack the Ripper, pictured after being murdered in her rented hovel in Millers Court, Dorset Street

from 1887 (the year he arrived back in England) to 1888 to familiarise himself with the East End (a vital part of the case); the dates show that Eppstein was in Turkey during the atrocities listed earlier, and there is no doubt that he would have become aware of the peculiar Turkish method of killings and mutilation, thus bringing these barbaric practices to England for the first time. He certainly fitted 'identikit' of being foreign looking - after 20 years in the hot Turkish climate - and he would have had access to clerical garb.

His connection with Whitechapel and Spitalfields can also be explained. During the late 19th century Christ Church, Spitalfields, started a policy of working very closely with other religions and among those with whom they had a strong connection was the Jewish Episcopal Chapel in Palestine Place of which Eppstein was lecturer!

Lectured

He also lectured quite frequently at Christ Church and at the United Methodist Free Church in *Hanbury Street,* opposite number 29, the murder location for Annie Chapman. Evidence of these lectures is shown in Parish Registers of the period which I found under a pile of rubble in Christ Church, and confirmed further by selected entries in the Christ Church Parish

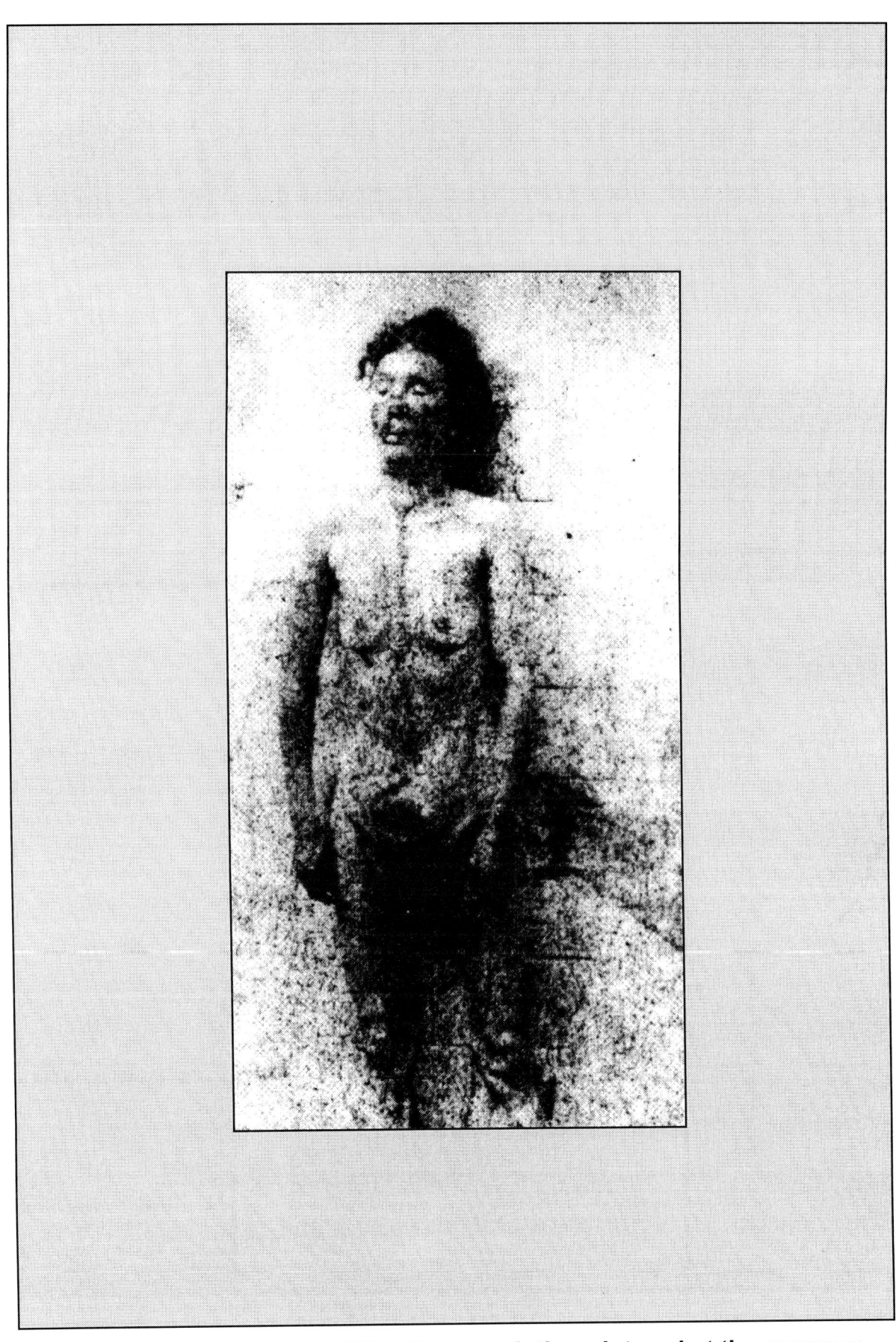

Catherine Eddowes, the Mitre Square victim, pictured at the morgue

magazine of the period. It all adds up to an impressive accusing finger against Eppstein.

Connection

But there is an even more interesting connection which was provided by my researches into Crockford's Clerical Directory. Directly underneath the entry for John Moses Eppstein (incidentally John is often changed to Jack) is an entry for his son William Charles Eppstein. And William Charles Eppstein was the Curate at *St Mary's, Spital Square* between 1887 and 1889! The chain of events is getting stronger.

Obviously with his son working in the district there would have been more reason for regular visits and thus acclimatising himself to the highways and byways of the district. In addition, after the glut on Mary Jane Kelly, John (Jack) Eppstein would have laid low automatically, and in the meantime his son moved from Whitechapel to a new position in Stowmarket thus no longer offering the same reason or opportunity for prowling the East End. This could explain why the killings of Jack the Ripper stopped so suddenly.

Bizarre

Why they started so suddenly can be explained by his years in Turkey, where women were (as in present day Middle East countries) required to show modesty. What a contrast Eppstein must have felt during his journeys around Whitechapel when he would have been faced with the most hideous sights of women by the thousand selling themselves on the streets for a few pennies. He could have seen his work as a Missionary in demand in a different way with the London 'unfortunates'.

Perhaps Sherlock Holmes was right with his comment: "As a rule, the more bizarre a thing is the less mysterious it proves to be..."!

Below: A copy of Mary Jane Kelly's death certificate

Who's Who?

Abberline, Chief Inspector, Frederick
(1843-1929)

The senior detective responsible for investigating the Ripper murders in 1888. He joined the Metropolitan Police in 1863 and was one of the fourteen divisional appointments made when the Criminal Investigation Department was formed in 1878. He was an acknowledged expert on London's East End, acquired when he served in the CID in Whitechapel.

Abberline was transferred to Scotland Yard in 1887 and was put in charge of the Whitechapel Murders investigation at the time of the Bucks Row killing. His detective team consisted of three inspectors and four sergeants. He was of a rather portly appearance described by Walter Dew, one of his young detectives, as a "gentle speaking" officer "who might easily have been mistaken for the manager of a bank or a solicitor."

In 1902 when Inspector George Godley arrested George Chapman (who was later hanged for the murders of his three wives), Abberline was reported as saying: "You've got Jack the Ripper at last!

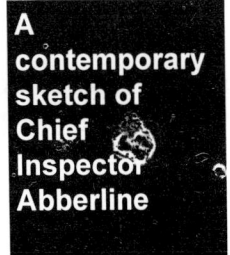

A contemporary sketch of Chief Inspector Abberline

Actor Michael Caine played the role of Chief Inspector Frederick Abberline in the Thames Television production of *Jack the Ripper* in 1988, in which Sir William Gull was named as the killer. (Photo courtesy of Thames TV)

He was promoted Detective Chief Inspector in 1889 and retired from the police force in 1892, moving to Bournemouth.

When the Ripper investigation closed, Abberline's team of detectives presented him with a handsome walking stick, the knob of which was carved in the form of a human head. The stick is displayed in a cabinet at the Police College, Bramshill, with an explanatory note which suggests that Abberline favoured the theory that an alleged Russian anarchist living in London was the suspect.

Albert Victor, HRH Prince (Duke of Clarence)

(1864-1892)

Eldest son of the Prince and Princess of Wales, known as Prince Albert Victor, or 'Eddy' to his friends, until he was created Duke of Clarence and Avondale in 1890. He was known to Ripperologists simply as Clarence. Grandson to Queen Victoria and heir presumptive to the English throne, he was engaged to be married to Princess Mary of Teck, who eventually became Queen Mary, wife of George V, after marrying Albert Victor's brother.

Six weeks before the set date for the marriage, 'Eddy' died of pneumonia, aged 28, following a bout of influenza. His affairs were linked to those of James Kenneth Stephen, his tutor at Cambridge University, who also died less than three weeks after the Duke of Clarence.

Known as 'Collar and Cuffs' after his exaggerated dress style, the prince has had a web of intrigue spun around him starting with the Cleveland Street Scandal of 1889 when he was alleged to have frequented a male brothel at 29 Cleveland Street.

His tutor has also been proposed as a candidate for Jack the Ripper, but the Duke of Clarence allegation has prompted wide publicity since it was first mooted in 1970 that 'Eddy' was the instigator of the Ripper murders. In the

The Duke of Clarence in a well known pose which gave rise to his 'Collar and Cuffs' nickname

article, by the late Dr. Thomas Stowell, the author referred to him as simply 'S', though the biographical details left no one in any doubt as to whom Stowell was referring. Several writers, notably American Frank Spierling and the late Stephen Knight both wove complex tales around the claim, though both theories fall far short of producing any actual evidence.

The theories involved claims of an official cover up in a plot to dispel a constitutional crisis after 'Eddy' allegedly secretly married a Roman Catholic who later gave birth to his child.

An unusual alibi! At the time of the Ripper scare Eddy was planting this tree in Tatton Park, Cheshire, England, while staying with the influential Tatton family, as the small plaque confirms

Anderson, Sir Robert

1841-1918

Appointed Assistant Commissioner of the Metropolitan Police and CID chief on September 1, 1888, when the Ripper scare was at its height.

His absence abroad on sick leave at the start of the Ripper scare excited criticism from the press, and on his recall the Home Secretary Henry Matthews told him he held Anderson responsible for catching the killer. He failed in this task, but crime in the Metropolitan area declined during his time in office.

He retired from office in May 1901 and died in 1918. He always believed he knew who Jack the Ripper was and wrote: "...I am tempted to disclose the identity of the murderer and of the pressman who wrote that letter...But no public benefit would result from such a course, and the traditions of my old department would suffer."

It appeared that Sir Robert's accusation was made against John Pizer, also known as Leather Apron, who was interviewed by police but later released for lack of evidence.

Barnett, Rev. Samuel A

1846-1904

The Vicar of St Judes, Commercial Street, Whitechapel, he was a pioneering social reformer known locally as the 'Saint of Whitechapel' because of his work with the East End poor. In 1885 he founded Toynbee Hall, the universities settlement in Spitalfields which still stands on Commercial Street.

In a letter to *The Times*, he wrote that the "Whitechapel horrors will not be in vain if at last the public conscience awakes to consider the life which those horrors reveal."

Barnett and his wife, Henrietta, campaigned for the abolition of the slaughter houses in Aldgate and argued that the daily slaughtering of animals in the heart of Whitechapel brutalised the population. His campaigning also succeeded in having some of the district's worst lodging houses in Flower and Dean Street demolished and replaced with new six-storey tenements, which have themselves now been demolished.

Baxter, Wynne E.

1844-1920

Coroner for the South East Division of Middlesex, he conducted three of the inquests on the Ripper's victims. A man of independent outlook, he did not shirk from criticising the authorities if necessary. He opened the inquest

on Mary Nichols on September 1, 1888, at the Working Lads' Institute in Whitechapel, which overlapped with the inquest on Annie Chapman who was killed on September 8. He believed the East End was in the grip of mass murder and linked the Nichols and Chapman deaths with those of Emma Smith and Martha Turner (or Tabram) who he was also investigating.

Baxter also held the inquest into the death of Elizabeth Stride which opened on October 20, 1888, and was soon famous for his graphic descriptions of how the various killings had been carried out by Jack the Ripper.

There was severe criticism that Baxter was not allowed to conduct the inquest into the murder of Millers Court victim Mary Jane Kelly, the task being given to Dr. Roderick Macdonald who hurried the inquiry through in record time. It has given rise to speculation of an official cover up.

Pictured, left, is the Whitechapel Lads' Institute in the 1880s, and, above, as it looks today with the upper facade almost totally unchanged

Blackwell, Dr. Frederick

1851-1900

A local physician who was called to examine the body of Elizabeth Stride in Berner Street on September 30, 1888. When he arrived at 1.16am the body was still warm and he estimated that the killing had taken place within the past 30 minutes, and also concluded that from the position of the body Stride's throat had been cut while she was lying on the ground.

He carried out the post-mortem examination with Dr. George Bagster Phillips, the police surgeon.

Bruises on the victim's shoulders suggested that while she may willingly have lain on the ground her assailant applied pressure to pin her down while he cut her throat. There was no evidence of any gagging or mutilations apart from the throat wound. Blackwell was also asked to examine a knife found in the vicinity but was inclined to rule it out as the murder weapon.

Chandler, Inspector Joseph

An H-Division Inspector of the Metropolitan Police on duty at Commercial Street Police Station when the discovery was reported of Annie Chapman's body in the backyard of 29 Hanbury Street. He sent for the divisional police surgeon Dr. Bagster Phillips and then hurried to the crime scene where he cleared the area of waiting people so a proper examination could be made of the victim and the murder location.

He noted a leather apron near the tap in the yard and noted that there was no evidence of any struggle of any bloodstains outside the yard.

In his report Chandler recorded that the body was identified by Timothy Donovan, a lodging-house keeper from nearby Dorset Street.

Chapman, Annie
1843-1888

Also known as Annie Sievey or 'Dark Annie', this 45 years old prostitute was murdered on September 8, 1888, at 29 Hanbury Street, and is today regarded as the second victim of the killer, though some authors regard her killing as his third because they include Martha Turner as the first.

Her body was found in the backyard of the house by John Davis on his way to work. She was lying flat on her back with  her throat cut and horrific mutilations inflicted on her body. Detectives found no evidence of any struggle but there were reports of blood splashes on the nearby fence, and oddments found on the ground, including part of an envelope, a comb and paper case, a couple of pills wrapped in paper and some copper coins.

Annie Chapman had been living in 35 Dorset Street, apart from her husband. Timothy Donovan, the lodging house deputy, told the inquest that Annie implored him not to let her bed when she left 35 Dorset Street on the day she was murdered. She was last seen alive, the worse for drink, walking towards Spitalfields Church a few hours before her death. Dr Phillips thought she had been dead about two hours when he examined the body at 6.30am.

Chapman, George
1865-1903

Born in Poland as Severin Klosowski but took the name of Chapman  after he married a woman by the name of Annie Chapman (no relation to the Ripper victim) in 1893.

It was as George Chapman that he was hanged in 1903 after being convicted of murder by poison. Inspector Abberline is said to have commented after Chapman's arrest by his collegue Chief Inspector George Godley "You've got Jack the Ripper at last!" Abberline is said to have later withdrew his comment but the damage had been done and some writers believe that Chapman/klosowski was indeed Jack the Ripper despite using a totally different *modus operandi* for the three murders he later committed and for which he was hanged.

Klosowski is thought to have come to England some time early in 1888 and worked in Whitechapel as a barber's assistant, at one time working in George Yard, close to the murder site of Martha Turner.

Cox, Mary Ann

One of the Dorset Street community of prostitutes, she was was a witness in the Kelly case. She told Inspector Abberline that she saw Mary Kelly at about 11.45pm on the night she was murdered, in the company of a man.

She described the man as aged about thirty six years old, about five feet five inches tall, with a fair, blotchy complexion. He had side whiskers and a thick carroty moustache; he wore shabby dark clothes and a black felt hat and was carrying a quart of beer.

Cox said that when she returned to Millers Court at about 1am she heard Kelly singing "Only a violet I plucked from my mother's grave", but when she returned again at 3am all was quiet and there was no light in number 13.

Cream, Dr. Thomas Neill

1850-1892

Notorious poisoner who committed murder in Britain and the United States and whom some believed to be Jack the Ripper. This accusation was based on his alleged statement on the scaffold, "I am Jack the..." just before the trap was sprung. James Billinghan, the hangman, is said to have sworn that these were Cream's dying words.

The story has been discredited on the simple grounds that at the time of the Jack the Ripper murders in London, Cream was serving a ten year sentence in Joliet prison in the USA and was not released until 1891.

Cross, Charles

A Carter from Bethnal Green who discovered the body of Mary Ann Nichols in Bucks Row, Whitechapel, on August 31, 1888. He was walking down Bucks Row on his way to work at about 3.45am when, by the light of a distant gas lamp, he saw a bundle lying partly on the pavement which he thought was a lost tarpaulin. On closer examination, however, he discovered it was a woman whom he thought was drunk. It was only when he was joined moments later by Robert Paul, another passing workman, that they discovered Nichols was bleeding from the throat and ran towards Brady Street where they met Police Constable John Neil who raised the alarm.

Cullen, Tom

American journalist and writer who worked in London for several years as a correspondent for a US news syndicate. In 1965 his book *Autumn of Terror* appeared in which he named Montague John Druitt as Jack the Ripper. He appears to have drew his source material from notes written by Sir Melville Macnaughton, Chief Constable and Head of the CID at Scotland Yard. His theory was received with caution by Ripper experts, but some believe (author Daniel Farson among them) that Druitt was indeed the killer.

Davies, Dr. Morgan

He was accused of being Jack the Ripper by Dr. Roslyn D'Onston Stephenson in a statement made to Scotland Yard on December 26, 1888.

It was alleged that Davies gave a realistic simulation of the way in which the Ripper took his victims. There is no evidence that Dr. Davies was regarded as a suspect by the police.

Davis, John

The elderly car-man who worked at Spitalfields Market and who discovered the body of Annie Chapman. He lived on the third floor of 29 Hanbury Street with his wife and three sons.

He was preparing to leave for work shortly before 6am on Saturday, September 8, when he paid a visit to the back yard and found the corpse. He rushed to Commercial Street Police Station to report the discovery to Inspector Chandler. In his evidence at Chapman's inquest, Davis confirmed that the front and yard doors of the house were frequently left open all night.

Dew, Chief Inspector Walter

1863-1947

The policeman who acquired fame in 1910 after arresting wife-killer Dr. Crippen, he was a rookie

detective in 1888 and was present at Millers Court when Mary Kelly's body was found. In his autobiography he wrote: "What I saw when I pushed back an old coat and peeped through a broken pane of glass into the sordid little room which Kelly called her home, was too harrowing to be described."

Dew always believed that Jack the Ripper was shielded by someone in the community and dismissed the idea that the murderer was medically skilled.

Diemschutz, Louis

Traveller in cheap costume jewellery who lived at 40 Berner Street and was steward of the International Working Men's Educational Club which had premises on the first floor. He

discovered the body of Elizabeth Stride at about 1am on September 30, 1888, when he returned home from market.

He later told the inquest: "I perhaps should not have noticed the body if my pony had not shied".

Druitt, Montague John

1857-1888

Born in Dorset the son of a doctor, Druitt's name came to the attention of writer Daniel Farson in

1959 and eventually emerged as the prime murder suspect, though it did not appear in print for the first time until Tom Cullen's book *Autumn of Terror* was published. The basis for suspecting Druitt as the Ripper is the reference made to him by Sir Melville Macnaughton in his notes written in 1894.

In the course of his text Macnaughton mentioned the names of three men and Druitt was one of them.

Macnaughton wrote: "I have little doubt but that his own family believed him to have been the murderer."

Druitt committed suicide by drowning himself in the river Thames and his body was found on December 31, 1888.

Above is part of The Minories in the East End of London where some investigators believe Montague John Druitt sheltered after the Ripper killings

The building pictured left is the former Bishopsgate Police Station in the City of London where Catherine Eddowes had been locked up for drunkenness. Shortly afterwards she was released and walked to her death at the hands of Jack the Ripper in nearby Mitre Square, which is pictured as it looked in the 1960s, almost unchanged from 1888

Eddowes, Catherine
1842-1888

Also known as Kate Kelly, Eddowes was murdered in Mitre Square between 1.30am and 1.45am on Sunday, September 30, 1888. She was Jack the Ripper's second victim that night and the fourth in the series.

Eddowes, a mother of three, was separated from her husband and, at the time of her death, was living with labourer John Kelly at 6 Fashion Street, Whitechapel. On the eve of her murder she was found drunk in Aldgate and taken to Bishopsgate Police Station to sober up.

She was released about 12.30am and was found 90 minutes later by PC 881 Watkins who was patrolling Mitre Square. Her throat was cut and her body mutilated, and her uterus and left kidney were found to be missing from her body. A kidney was later sent through the post to George Lusk, head of the Whitechapel Vigilante Committee.

In 1966 contemporary sketches of Eddowes body were found in the London Hospital basement where they had lain forgotten for 80 years.

Farson, Daniel

Journalist, television interviewer and playwright who named Montague John Druitt as his candidate for Jack the Ripper in his book published in 1972. Farson attributed his interest in the subject to Colin Wilson whom he interviewed in television in 1956.

He included the subject of Jack the Ripper in his programme *Farson's Guide to the British*. His research for the programme led him to Lady Aberconway, daughter of CID chief Sir Melville Macnaughton, who told him of the existence of her father's notes in which he named M.J. Druitt as a suspect.

Godley, George
Chief Inspector

As a sergeant in the Metropolitan Police, he worked with Inspector Frederick Abberline and the Ripper murder investigation team. Years later Godley gained distinction as the officer who arrested Ripper suspect George Chapman for a totally separate series of killings.

Gladstone, William
Ewart
1809-1898

Four times British Prime Minister during the reign of Queen Victoria, alternating in office with Lord Salisbury. He was a highly religious man who was said to have regarded life as a branch of personal religion. He is best remembered for giving his name to a piece of travelling luggage, but his eccentric behaviour of walking the streets of the East End at night talking to prostitutes is less well known. He too has been named as a Ripper suspect.

Gull, Sir William
Withey
1816-1890

Distinguished doctor with a West End practice who counted members of nobility and the Royal Family among his patients. After being created a baronet in 1872 he became regular physician to the Prince of Wales and was subsequently appointed Physician in Ordinary to Queen Victoria. The suggestion that Gull was Jack the Ripper was first made by Walter Sickert, the impressionist painter, and was later woven into a tale of conspiracy in high places by the late Stephen Knight in his book *Jack the Ripper: The Final Solution*, published in 1976.

Critics of the Gull theory have argued that a man of 72, enfeebled by a stroke in the previous year would not have been physically able to carry out the murders. According to official records Sir William Gull died of a cerebral haemorrhage in January 1890 and was buried at Thorpe-le-Soken in Essex.

Harvey, Maria

A prostitute who shared Mary Kelly's lodgings at 13 Millers Court and who ousted her lover Joseph Barnett. Kelly was in arrears with her rent and might have been persuaded to take in Harvey to contribute to the rent since Barnett was unemployed. It has also been suggested that the two women were lesbians and this is what caused the argument between Kelly and Barnett on October 30, 1888. Objects were thrown and a window was broken with the outcome that Barnett left.

Harvey also later left to live at 3 New Court, Dorset Street, and left some clothes behind and it has been suggested that the traces of female clothing in the fire-grate of the murder room were the result of the murderer burning them to provide illumination.

Hutchinson, George

Labourer lodging at the Victoria Home, Commercial Street who made a highly detailed statement to the police of a man he saw in the company of Mary Jane Kelly on the night she was murdered. Part of his statement said: "He had a kind of small parcel in his left hand with a kind of strap round it. I stood against the lamp of the Queens Head Public House and watched him. They both then came past me and the man hung down his head with his hat over his eyes. I stooped down and looked him in the face. He looked at me stern. They both went into Dorset Street...They both then went up the Court together. I then went to the Court to see if I could see them but could not."

Hutchinson made his statement after the coroner Dr. Roderick Macdonald had brought the inquest of Kelly to a singularly speedy conclusion so the statement was never presented in evidence.

Mary Jane Kelly with her killer as described by George Hutchinson in a contemporary sketch

Isenschmid, Joseph

Pork butcher who was arrested as a Ripper suspect on September 12, 1888, in the wake of the Annie Chapman murder and the hunt for 'Leather Apron'. Isenschmid attracted attention because of his odd comings and goings at his lodgings in 60 Milford Road, Holloway. Shortly after he was certified as a dangerous lunatic and confined to Bow Infirmary Asylum, during which time further Ripper murders took place, thus clearing him of any connection with the killings.

Kelly, Mary Jane
1863-1888

Twenty five years old prostitute who became Jack the Ripper's last victim. She was murdered in 13 Millers Court, Dorset Street, on November 9, 1888 and her body was subjected to horrific mutilations. The murder was discovered by Thomas Bowyer, her landlord's assistant, when he called for payment of her rent arrears. Born in Ireland and one in a family of seven, Mary Jane married a Welsh miner when she was 16 years of age. Her husband was killed in a mine explosion and she took to prostitution while still a teenager, moving to London in 1884 and later to France where she took to calling herself Marie Jeanette. She returned to London and drifted to the East End where she started living with Joe Barnett, a porter at Billingsgate Market, who it has been suggested murdered her and was in fact Jack the Ripper!

After the horrific murder the remains of Mary Kelly were buried in Leytonstone Cemetery on November 19, the coffin being inscribed *Marie Jeanette Kelly, died November 9, 1888, aged 25 years.*

The cost of her funeral was paid for by Mr. H. Wilton, who for 50 years had been sexton of St Leonard's Church in Shoreditch where a funeral service to Kelly was held.

In 1988 local Ripperologist John Morrison, who lived only yards from Mary's grave, paid for a headstone to be erected in her memory, a tribute which was not well received by many local people who did not share his enthusiasm for remembering the Ripper's last victim.

Lees, Robert James
1849-1931

Described in a Sunday newspaper article in 1895 as a "philanthropist and advanced labour leader", he was well connected and said to be a friend of many of the leading political figures of his day but it was his clairvoyant powers which brought him into the Ripper story. Lees was credited with arranging seances for Queen Victoria to assist her endeavours to contact her departed consort Prince Albert.

The popular story is that Lees dreamed of some of the Ripper crimes in advance of their happening and persuaded the police to let him take them to the murderer. The man he identified proved to be a doctor living in a fashionable house in London's West End. In due course, he was certified as a lunatic and placed in an asylum.

The story has taken several courses over the years, and in the 1988 TV series *Jack the Ripper*, starring Michael Caine, the character of Lees was a main feature of the film with the fashionable doctor eventually being identified as Dr. William Gull.

Llewellyn,
Dr. Rees Ralph
1849-1921

Physician called from his home at 152 Whitechapel Road to the scene of the first Ripper murder in Bucks Row on August 31, 1888. The doctor found Mary Ann Nichols lying dead with her throat cut. He ordered her body to be taken to the Old Montague Street Workhouse Mortuary where he subsequently carried out a post mortem examination.

Dr. Llewellyn found that the body had been stripped and washed before he arrived, thus destroying important evidence. He also found what had been apparent in the gloom of the early morning, that the woman had been extensively mutilated. The doctor's assessment of the injuries were that the murderer must have possessed some rough anatomical knowledge and he stated that the mutilations were "deftly and fairly skilfully performed."

Lusk, George

1839-1919

East End builder and Chairman of the Whitechapel Vigilance Committee founded by local tradesmen in the wake of Annie Chapman's murder. After the 'double event' of September 20, 1888, Lusk presented a petition to Queen Victoria on behalf of the inhabitants asking her Government to offer a reward for the capture of the Whitechapel murderer.

On October 16, 1888, Lusk received a brown paper wrapped package through the post at his home in Alderney Road, Mile End. The parcel contained part of a human kidney, thought to have been the organ removed from the body of Catherine Eddowes, together with a note addressed *From Hell*.
The note read:

From Hell,
Mr Lusk, sir, I send you have the kidne I took from one woman,
prasarved it to you,
tother piece I fried and ate it; it was very nise. I may send you the bloody knif that
took it out if you only wate a whil longer.
signed,
Catch me when you can,
Mishter Lusk.

C.M. MacLeod, a Canadian graphologist writing in the *Criminologist* in August 1968, believed the letter was likely to be genuine.
While it was the letter accompanying the unwanted gift of a kidney sent to Lusk which excited all the attention, he had received a letter signed *Jack the Ripper* only four days previously, and this was the start of the infamous name.

Macnaughton, Sir Melville

1853-1921

Chief Constable and Head of the CID at Scotland Yard between 1889 and 1903 and Assistant Commissioner of the Metropolitan Police from 1903 to 1913. The youngest of 15 children, he was educated at Eton and in 1873 went to India to manage his father's properties in Bengal. He met James Monro, the Inspector-General of the Bengal Police and a future Commissioner of the Metropolitan Police, and the two men became life-long friends.
He published his autobiography *Days of My Years* in 1914 and stated that in his opinion the Ripper's brain gave way after the Millers Court murder and he committed suicide.

Matters, Leonard

1881-1951

Australian journalist and MP who wrote the first full-length book on Jack the Ripper, published in 1929 and titled *The Mystery of Jack the Ripper*, which was once called "the most coherent, plausible and acceptable explanation", later commentators condemned the book as a fictional account of the murders with his suspect being a man he called 'Dr Stanley' who killed the East End whores after his son became infected with syphillis. His mission completed, 'Dr Stanley' went to Argentina where he confessed to an old pupil that he was Jack the Ripper.
The first half of Matters book was in fact well-written and researched and gave a good, accurate, account of the Whitechapel killings, but, unfortunately for posterity, his 'Dr. Stanley' theory in the latter part of the book spoilt it because of the lack of backing evidence.

Matthews, Henry

1826-1913

Barrister who served as Home Secretary during the period of the Ripper murders. He was the first Roman catholic to be made a Cabinet Minister since the passing of the Emancipation

Act. Although he was regarded as an able lawyer he was not judged to be adept at managing people and he found Metropolitan Police Commissioner Sir Charles Warren hard to handle and presided over a series of resignations and appointments.

First, he accepted the departure of James Monro, the Assistant Commissioner who found it impossible to work with Warren, and appointed his successor Sir Robert Anderson. Then he accepted Warren's resignation at the time of the Kelly murder and reinstated Monro to the force as Commissioner.

Sir Melville Macnaughton

Home Secretary Henry Matthews

M'Carthy, John

Lodging house keeper who kept a chandler's shop at 27 Dorset Street and rented rooms in the district to the local prostitutes. His tenants were known as *M'Carthy's Rents* and one of these was Mary Kelly. She had not paid her rent for several weeks and was 35 shillings (£1.62p) in arrears.

At about 10.45am on November 9, 1888, M'Carthy sent his assistant Thomas Bowyer to see Kelly and ask for her outstanding rent money. Obtaining no reply, he peered through the broken window and saw Kelly's mutilated corpse lying on the bed.

Rushing back to bring M'Carthy to the scene, Bowyer later said: "The sight we saw I cannot drive away from my mind. It looked more like the work of a devil than of a man."

McCormick, Donald
1911-

Journalist with extensive knowledge of foreign affairs who developed the theory that Jack the Ripper was the Russian barber surgeon Dr. Alexander Pedachenko. He first published his account in 1959 in a book titled *The Identity of Jack the Ripper*, which appeared in a revised edition in 1970.

The greatest drawback to McCormick's theory is the impossibility of checking his more important source material.

McKenzie, Alice

1849-1889

Known as 'Clay Pipe Annie' Mckenzie was murdered in the early hours of July 17, 1889 in

Castle Alley, Whitechapel. Her throat had been cut and there were superficial wounds to her abdomen. Rumours spread that Jack the Ripper had struck again, but Dr. Phillips carried out the post mortem examination and in his report he gave his opinion that the injuries

inflicted on Alice were not consistent with those associated with the Ripper crimes, but for some unknown reason Sir Robert Anderson called for a second opinion from Dr. Thomas Bond who disagreed with Dr. Phillips' findings. Bond reported that he saw "murder evidence of a similar design to the former Whitechapel murders". Most Ripper experts agree with the findings of Dr. Phillips whose report is unique in being lodged in the official Ripper files, for he more than anyone would recognise the trademark of Jack the Ripper, having examined four of the earlier victims.

Monro, James

1838-1920

Assistant Commissioner at Scotland Yard under Sir Charles Warren who resigned on August 31, 1888 when the Ripper murders began and was appointed Warren's successor as Commissioner on December 3, 1888, after the murders had finished.

Monro was born in Edinburgh and spent all but six years of his working life abroad. He had served in India for 26 years and was Inspector-General of the Bengal Police when he was appointed Chief of CID and Assistant Commissioner at Scotland Yard in 1884. He was a highly rated officer and though by

some to have been the only man likely to track down Jack the Ripper.

After his appointment as Commissioner he campaigned successfully for reforms in the police service.

Neil, John
PC 97J

Called to the scene of the Ripper's first murder victim. While patrolling his beat in Bucks Row, Whitechapel on August 31, 1888, he was summoned by Charles Cross who had found the body of Mary Ann Nichols at 3.45am.

Neil, an officer of 20 years experience, summoned assistance and sent for Dr. Ralph Llewellyn who lived nearby. PC Neil said that, allowing for the inspection of premises on his beat, he must have passed the murder scene about 30 minutes before the crime was discovered.

Netley, John
Charles

1860-1903

Coachman who assisted Sir William Gull on his sorties into the East End as Jack the Ripper,

according to some theories. He was named as one of the murderous trio by Walter Sickert, the third member being named as Sir Robert Anderson, who said that he hired out his own coach and was employed by Prince Albert Victor to take him to secret meetings with his lover Annie Elizabeth Crook.

A researcher working on a BBC programme about Jack the Ripper discovered that a John Netley, aged 43, died in a road accident in Regent's Park in September 1903, having been thrown from the vehicle he was driving and died under the hooves of one of the horses. The theory was told in greater detail in Stephen Knight's book *Jack the Ripper: The Final Solution.*

Nichols, Mary Ann
1846-1888

Generally acknowledged as the first victim of Jack the Ripper, her body was found in Bucks Row, Whitechapel, on August 31, 1888. Her throat had been cut and there were extensive mutilations to her abdomen which led Dr. Ralph Llewellyn to conclude that the killer possessed some medical skill. Nichols was buried on September 7, 1888, and the hearse bore her remains down Hanbury Street where, the next day, the second Ripper victim was to meet her death. The residents of Bucks Row were so upset by Nichols' killing that they petitioned to change the name of the street to Durward Street, the name it still has today.

Odell, Robin
1935-

Author of the theory that the facts of the Ripper murders pointed to a ritual Jewish slaughterman as the likely candidate. He argued that the decisive cutting of the victim's throat while lying on the ground, which proved to be a hallmark of the Ripper's technique, was a method employed by the *shochet* in the ritual slaughter of animals.

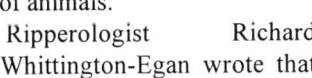

Ripperologist Richard Whittington-Egan wrote that Odell's account was a "reasoned, and reasonable, interpretation of the Ripper's psychopathology together with a feasible theory as to the nature of his occupation."

Ostrog, Michael
1833-?

The third suspect named by Sir Melville Macnaughton in his notes on the murders. He described the suspect as "a Russian doctor, and a convict, who was frequently detained in a lunatic

asylum as a homicidal maniac."

Ostrog was an enigmatic figure with a string of supposed aliases, and his name has been linked with other Russian suspects.

Phillips, Dr. George Bagster

Metropolitan Police Divisional Surgeon who lived at 2 Spital Square in the heart of Spitalfields. Of all the medical men involved in the investigation of the Ripper murders, Dr. Phillips, with 43 years experience as a police surgeon, was one of the most experienced, and he became the most familiar with Jack the Ripper's methods of killing and mutilation. He was called to the scene of three of the murders and was present at the post mortem examination of four victims.

Pizer, John

A Polish Jew who lived and worked in the East End and came under suspicion during the hue and cry for 'Leather Apron' following the murder of Mary Ann Nichols. Pizer, a boot finisher by trade, wore the traditional leather apron and also worked with knives. Pizer, of 22 Mulberry Street, was arrested and questioned by detectives but later released. He appeared as a witness at the Chapman inquest and was completely exonerated by coroner Wynne Baxter.

Smith, Sir Henry
1835-1921

Acting Commissioner of the City of London Police at the time of the Jack the Ripper murders, he had two claims to fame. He boasted in his memoirs that no one living knew more about the murders than he did, and claimed to be the only man to command both the City Police and the Metropolitan Police forces for a state occasion in London. He was in command of the investigation into the murder of Catherine Eddowes in Mitre Square on September 30, 1888, this being the only killing in the series which took place in the City of London Police jurisdiction.

He was angry that Eddowes had been released from custody in Bishopsgate Police Station after being drunk and was allowed to wander to Mitre Square where she met her dreadful fate at the hands of the Ripper. Her body was found at 1.45am by PC Watkins.

Smith, PC William

Beat constable who patrolled Berner Street on the night that Elizabeth Stride was murdered. He told the inquest that he saw Stride in Berner Street at about 12.30pm or 12.40pm. She was talking to a man who carried a parcel about eighteen inches long wrapped in newspaper. He described him as about five feet seven inches, wearing dark clothes, a cutaway coat and a deerstalker hat.

J.K. Stephen
1859-1892

Son of Sir James Fitzjames Stephen the Victorian judge who resigned the bench in 1891 because of mental illness, and a cousin of Virginia Woolf the author who also suffered with mental anguish resulting in her suicide, J.K. Stephen was a handsome young man acknowledged to be among the ablest of his

generation. He was named as Jack the Ripper by author Michael Harrison in his book *Clarence* on the theory that James Kenneth Stephen was driven to murder by feelings of jealousy which erupted after severing his connection with Prince Albert Victor, to whom he was tutor.

Stephenson, Roslyn D'Onston
1841-?

He was a black magic practitioner suspected of being Jack the Ripper by W.T. Stead, editor of the *Pall Mall Gazette*. He was also suspected by Aleister Crowley, a professional occulist who claimed to know more about the killings than perhaps he did.

Stephenson even made a statement of his own to Scotland Yard officers in which he drew attention to suspicions which he held against a Dr. Morgan Davies! Stephenson was described as a bohemian figure and he lived up to his reputation when he disappeared. Inquiries have since failed to find his final whereabouts or date of death.

Stewart, William

Brixton artist who turned his attention to solving the Whitechapel murders and in 1939 published his book *Jack the Ripper: A New Theory*, which was illustrated with pictures taken in 1938 of Whitechapel and Spitalfields as well as pictures sketched by himself from contemporary reports of 1888.

He also built miniature sets of the murder scenes which were also photographed and published in the book, one of the most sought after publications by Ripperologists. His theory was that the killer was in fact a female midwife - or Jill the Ripper, not Jack!

Stride, Elizabeth 'Long Liz'

1843-1888

Forty-five years old prostitute, also known as 'Long Liz', who became Jack the Ripper's third victim and his first on the night of the so-called 'Double Event' on September 30, 1888. She was found murdered in Dutfield's Yard, Whitechapel, at about 1am by Louis Diemschutz, steward of the International Working Men's Educational Club.

She was the only victim to be murdered without the normal Ripper trademark of mutilations afterwards, probably because he was disturbed by the arrival of Diemschutz.

Turner, Martha

1853-1888

Also known as Martha Tabram, she was a married woman who also earned her living as a prostitute in the East End, and she died at the hands of an unknown assailant on August 6, 1888, and has been considered a Ripper victim (some say his first), by some authors and crime enthusiasts, but most Ripper experts now tend to dismiss this as unlikely.

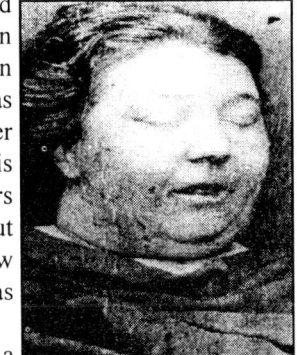

Turner was attacked on a landing at 35 George Yard Buildings and died from a knife attack in which she sustained 39 stab wounds in the chest. Her throat had not been cut, which was a hallmark of the Jack the Ripper murders,

Swanson, Chief Inspector Donald

1848-1924

Senior officer at Scotland Yard's Criminal Investigation Department whose official reports on a number of important incidents during the murder series has been made public.

His accounts of the Hanbury Street murder (Annie Chapman) and the double event on September 30 (Elizabeth Stride and Catherine Eddowes) were included in Stephen Knight's book *Jack the Ripper: The Final Solution*.

As late as 1896 he was writing reports on letters purporting to have been written by Jack the Ripper which were still being received by Scotland Yard. The fact that one of his reports dated October 18, 1896, was annotated by Sir Melville Macnaughton and sent to the Commissioner for his attention is taken as significant because it shows that a number of senior police officers thought the case was still very much open.

Victoria, Queen

1819-1901

Her Majesty's Jubilee Year of 1887 was followed by a year distinguished for its series of sensational murders in the East End of London. She was certainly not amused and she demanded action with letters to the Home Secretary and the Prime Minister Lord Salisbury.

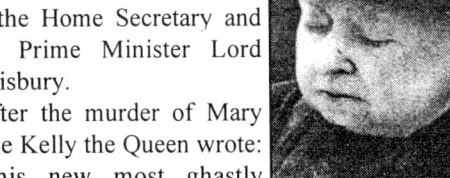

After the murder of Mary Jane Kelly the Queen wrote: "This new most ghastly murder shows the absolute necessity for some decided action."

Warren, Sir Charles

1840-1927

In March, 1886, Sir Charles Warren was plucked from a military career and appointed Commissioner of the London Metropolitan Police at Scotland Yard. Many harsh things were said about his term of office and a smouldering quarrel between him and his

Assistant Commissioner James Monro resulted in Monro resigning.

Warren was made a popular scapegoat for the failure of Scotland Yard to catch Jack the Ripper and he was frequently lampooned by the press. He was simply the wrong man for the job, and his attempt to bring military discipline to his men was frowned upon and did nothing to improve their motivation.

On November 8, 1888, the day before the Ripper's final bloodbath in Millers Court, Sir Charles Warren resigned, and, ironically, he was succeeded as Commissioner by James Monro.

After his resignation Sir Charles returned to a military career and served in various campaigns in the Boer War and was promoted to a full General in 1904 and spent an active retirement until his death in 1927.

Whittington-Egan, Richard
1924-

Liverpool born biographer, journalist, broadcaster and crime writer, he published a series of articles in the *Contemporary Review* in the 1970s which later appeared in book form in 1975 under the title *A Casebook on Jack the Ripper.*

His writings are renowned among Ripperologists for their meticulous attention to detail, and as he admits: "I come, not as an innovator, but as a commentator."

He carefully examined all the theories put forward upto the time of his book being published and his opinion on Jack the Ripper theories is still highly respected.

Wilson, Colin
1931-

Prolific author of works on crime related subjects, philosophy and the occult, his name first attracted public attention on 1956 when his first book *The Outsider* was published to wide acclaim. He has admitted a fascination for the subject of Jack the Ripper since boyhood and though he had written many magazine articles about the murders his first full-length book on the subject *Jack the Ripper: Summing Up and Verdict,* which was written in co-operation with Ripper author Robin Odell, was not published until 1987.

Wilson noted that Jack the Ripper heralded a new type of crime which the Victorians had not recognised at that time, but which we now call a serial killer.

Winslow, Forbes
1844-1913

Dr. Winslow gave expert evidence in a number of murder cases in the Victorian era, and he was fascinated by the Jack the Ripper murders and he believed he could help Scotland Yard track down the killer. The Yard rejected his offers of help and he conducted his own investigations. He came to the conclusion that the Ripper was a  homicidal religious maniac seeking vengeance against prostitutes.

Dr. Winslow firmly believed that it was his investigation and not Scotland Yard's which caused the murders to stop after the killing of Mary Jane Kelly, driving him to leave Britain for Australia in 1889.

Author's Note: **This list is by no means complete and is intended only as a quick guide. For a much more comprehensive list it is recommended that Ripper enthusiasts should read the book *The Jack the Ripper A-Z* by Paul Begg, Martin Fido and Keith Skinner. (Headline Book Publishing)**

Photo Album

Old alleyways still survive in Whitechapel which would have been recognised by Jack the Ripper, who may even have escaped detection by using the one on the left leading into Whitechapel Road

The alleyway on the right is to be found just off Whitechapel Road, close to the murder sites

Pictured left is Durward Street, formerly Bucks Row, being rebuilt in 1996. The site of Mary Ann Nichols' murder is to the right of the building. Below is Hanbury Street in 1996 showing a brewery on the site of number 29, scene of Annie Chapman's murder

Bucks Row, scene of
Mary Ann Nichols' murder
pictured (left) in 1938,and
Hanbury Street, (below)
scene of Annie Chap-
man's murder. The arrows
show the actual murder
sites. Compare them with
the sites today!

This building was originally Commercial Street Police Station, and through these doors the murder of Annie Chapman was reported by John Davis who found her body in the yard of 29 Hanbury Street

The former retirement home of Chief Inspector Frederick Abbeline in Bournemouth, which is now a nursing home

This is the main entrance to Shoreditch Town Hall in London where the inquest into Mary Jane Kelly's death was held on the first floor on December 12, 1888

Christ Church, Spitalfields, which has been unused for services for many years, pictured today totally unchanged from the days of Jack the Ripper. At Mary Kelly's inquest witnesses stated they knew a particular time because they had heard Christ Church clock striking

Pictured in 1888 is the Rev. Hubert Scott, and his staff of Christ Church, Spital-fields. Was J.M. Eppstein, my Jack the Ripper suspect, one of those pictured!. Unfortunately nobody will ever know!

Pictured above is the old Scotland Yard HQ, the heart of the Ripper inquiry in 1888, while the more familiar New Scotland Yard building, pictured right, was not completed until 1890, two years after the killings. This building is now used by British Members of Parliament, with a new New Scotland Yard being opened in 1967 a mile away.

Pictured above is the grave of John McCarthy, landlord to Mary Jane Kelly, who is, coincidentally, buried in Leytonstone, close to her grave which is shown right with local Ripperologist John Morrison. John paid for a headstone for the last resting place of Mary (or Marie Jeanette as she liked to be called) despite opposition from local people. He is convinced she was killed by a former lover called James Kelly, who had escaped from Broadmoor Lunantic Asylum.

Author and Ghost Hunter Peter Underwood who is convinced the spirits of the Ripper victims still haunt the East End

The entrance to St Patrick's RC Cemetery, Leytonstone, London, last resting place of Mary Jane Kelly. She is buried in grave number 16, Row 67

This was once Dorset Street, Spital-fields, but is now a car park and extension of Spitalfields Market. Ripperologist John Morrison is seen indicating where the entrance to Millers Court on the right of the picture once stood.

Pictured right is London Hospital where photographs of some of the Ripper victims were discovered in the 1970s.

Below is pictured John Morrison (left) and Mark Galloway, two keen Ripperologists in John's own 'Murder Room' in his London home. Mark runs the Cloak & Dagger Club, devoted to the Ripper saga.

Televison and books have both covered the Jack the Ripper story in many different ways, but perhaps one of the most interesting and comprehensive programmes about the crimes was made in 1973 by the BBC when they made a series starring the superb partnership of Frank Windsor (above) as Superintendent John Watt, and Stratford Johns (right) as Superintendent Charlie Barlow. The series was based on the book *The Ripper File* by Elwyn Jones and John Lloyd, and first introduced the theory by Joseph Sickert about the Royal Family connection.

And finally...!

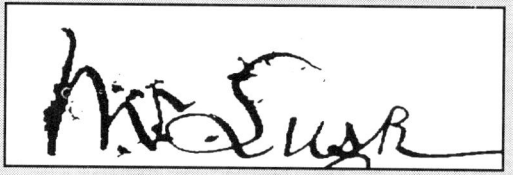

The letter at the top of the page was sent to George Lusk, Chairman of the Whitechapel Vigilante Committee, and is believed to have been one of the few authentic messages sent by Jack the Ripper. It is interesting to compare the handwriting sample, which experts believe was deliberately exaggerated, to the two samples of signatures from my prime suspect J.M. Eppstein, who preached sermons at Christ Church, Spitalfields, at a number of dates close to the murders. Readers can make up their own minds as to the similarity between the signatures and the handwriting of the letter to Mr. Lusk. If this gives food for thought to other Ripperologists, and allows further inquiries to be made into the background of Eppstein, then my task will be complete!

SELECT BIBLIOGRAPHY

Adam, Hargrave Lee: *Trial of George Chapman*. Hodge 1930.

Anderson, Sir Robert: *Criminals and Crime*. Nisbet 1907.

Anderson, Sir Robert: *The Lighter Side of my Official Life*. Hodder & Stoughton 1910.

Begg, Paul: *Jack the Ripper, The Uncensored Facts*. Robson Books, 1990.

Begg, Paul, Fido, Martin, and Skinner, Keith:
The Jack the Ripper A to Z. Headline 1991.

Beaumont, F.A.: *The Fiend of East London. The Fifty Most Amazing Crimes of the Last 100 Years*. Odhams 1936.

Camps, Professor Francis E. and Barber, Richard:
The Investigation of Murder. Michael Joseph 1966.

Cullen, Tom A.: *Autumn of Terror: Jack the Ripper, his Crimes and Times*. Bodley Head 1965. Fontana 1973.

Deacon, Richard: *A History of the British Secret Service*. Muller 1969.

Deacon, Richard: *A History of the Russian Secret Service*. Muller 1972.

Dew, Walter: *I Caught Crippen*. Blackie 1938.

Douglas, Arthur: *Will the Real Jack the Ripper*. Countryside Publications 1979.

Evans, Stewart & Gainey, Paul:
The Lodger, The Arrest & Escape of Jack the Ripper. Century Limited 1995.

Farson, Daniel: *Jack the Ripper*. Michael Joseph 1972.

Fairclough, Melvyn: *The Ripper & The Royals*, Gerald Duckworth, 1991.

Fido, Martin: *The Crimes, Detection, and Death of Jack the Ripper*, Orion Books, 1993.

Griffiths, Arthur George Frederick: *Mysteries of Police and Crime*. Cassell 1898.

Halsted, Dennis Gratwick: *Doctor in the Nineties*. Johnson 1959.

Harris, Melvin: *Jack the Ripper, The Bloody Truth*. Columbus Books, 1987.

Harris, Melvin: *The True Face of Jack the Ripper*, Michael O'Mara Books, 1994.

Harrison, Michael: *Clarence: the Life of the Duke of Clarence and Avondale*. W.H. Allen 1972

Harrison, Paul: *Jack the Ripper, The Mystery Solved*. Hale 1991.

Howells, Martin, and Skinner, Keith, *The Ripper Legacy*, Sidgwick & Jackson, 1987.

Jones, Elwyn: *The Ripper File*. Arthur Barker/Futura Publications 1975.

Knight, Stephen: *Jack the Ripper: The Final Solution*. Harrap 1976.

Lesson, Benjamin: *Lost London: The Memoirs of An East End Detective*. Stanley Paul 1934.

Le Queux, William: *Things I Know About Kings, Celebrities, and Crooks*. Nash & Grayson 1923.

MacLeod, C.M.: 'A Ripper Handwriting Analysis.' *Criminologist*. August 1968.

Macnaghten, Sir Melville L.:
Days of My Years. Arnold 1914

Marjoribanks, Edward:
The Life of Sir Edward Marshall Hall. Gollanez 1929.

Matters, Leonard W: *The Mystery of Jack the Ripper*. Hutchinson 1928.

McCormick, Donald: *The Identity of Jack the Ripper*. Jarrolds 1959.

Moore-Anderson, Arthur P,.: *Sir Robert Anderson and Lady Agnes Anderson*. Marshall, Morgan & Scott 1949.

Odell, Robin: *Jack the Ripper in Fact and Fiction*. Harrop, 1965.

Rumbelow, Donald: *The Complete Jack the Ripper*. W.H. Allen 1975, Star Books 1979.

Scott, Sir Harold: *The Concise Encyclopedia of Crime and Criminals*. Andre Deutsch 1961.

Smith, Sir Henry: *From Constable to Commissioner*. Chatto & Windus 1910.

Spiering, Frank: *Prince Jack*. Doubleday & Co. 1978.

Stewart, William: *Jack the Ripper: A New Theory*. Quality Press 1939.

Stowell, Thomas E. A.: 'Jack the Ripper - A Solution?' *Criminologist*. November 1970.

Thornbury, Walter: *Old London - The Tower & East End*. Alderman Press 1986.

Underwood, Peter: *Jack the Ripper, 100 Years of Mystery*. Blandford Press, 1987.

Wagner, Gillian: *Barnado*. Eyre & Spottiswoode 1980.

Whittington-Egan, Richard:
A Casebook on Jack the Ripper. Wildy & Sons 1975.

Wilson, Colin, & Odell, Robin: *Jack the Ripper, Summing Up and Verdict*. Bantam Press, 1987.

Subscribers

Aliffe Andy, Buckinghamshire.
Askew James & Son, Lancs, England.
Banner Mark, Wednesbury, West Midlands.
Bartley, Nigel, Hampshire, England.
Beadle E. Jeremy, Hertfordshire, England.
Bettany R., Norfolk, England.
Blackwell's Bookshop, Dorset, England.
Brady Robert, Atherton, Manchester.
Book Centre The, Herts, England.
Books for Students, Heathcote, Warwick, England.
Browns Books, Hull, England.
Chandler Louise, Cleethorpes, Lincolnshire.
Chick Edward W.G., British Columbia, Canada.
Chisholm Alex, Gwent, Wales.
Clarke Harvey, Taunton, Somerset, England.
Collins R.H., Bury St. Edmunds, England.
Corporation Of London Libraries, England.
Coventry Bookshop, England.
Crace Kevin F., Kent, England.
Cuerden Catherine, Ribbleton, Preston, Lancs.
Curtice Mark, Axbridge, Somerset, England.
Daniel Paul, London, England.
Deakin Karl, Liverpool, England.
Deben Bookshop, The, Suffolk, England.
Devlin Ted, Quebec, Canada.
Farries T.C. & Co., Dumfries, Scotland.
Fattig Timothy W., Missouri, USA.
Froggatt Dave, Birmingham, England.
Gage Barry, Cornwall, England.
Germanek R.J., Stoke-on-Trent, Staffordshire.
Gibb Jill, Peterborough, England.
Glasgow William, Glasgow, Scotland.
Gregg Wilf, Middlesex, England.
Haase Holger, Cork, Ireland.
Harris Neil, Birmingham, England.
Henry J. Gail, Lancaster, USA.
Hinton R., First Impressions, Llanelli, Wales.
Ives R.L., Tooting, London, England.
Janssen Stern Verlag, Dusseldorf, Germany.
Jeffries Gail, Leigh, Lancashire, England.
JMLS, Nottingham, England.

Johnstone J.D., York, England.
Laboy Yvette, New York, USA.
Lane Richard Northampton, England.
Lazell-Wood Janice, Essex, England.
Library & Information Services, Norfolk, England.
Library Processing Services, Warwick, England.
Luff Raymond, Surrey, England.
Marylebone Library, London, England.
McGrath Brendan, Dublin, Eire.
Michael, Dr. William P., Sweden.
Moffatt J.C., Ontario, Canada.
Morley Book Co., Leeds, England.
Morris Adrian, London, England.
Murder One, London, England.
Newton J.R., London, England.
Norfolk Library, Norwich, England.
Orchard Jane, Liverpool, England.
Porter C., Tunbridge Wells, Kent, England.
Rain B.J., Watford, Hertfordshire.
Richards A., Leicester, England.
Rothery S.T., Leeds, England.
Sayers Ralph, East Sussex, England.
Skinner Keith, Middlesex, England.
Smith Roger, Tardebigge, Worcestershire.
Smithkey John III , Canton, Ohio, USA.
Stanley Colin, Nottingham, England.
Stedman John, London, England.
Strachan Ross, Ayrshire, Scotland.
Stock Judith A, Connecticut, USA.
Thompson Anne M., Birmingham, England.
Tovell John, London, England.
Tranter P., Salisbury, Wiltshire, England.
Tully J.C.H., Altea, (Alicante), Spain.
Upton D.E., Liverpool, England.
Vince Michael, Buckingham, England.
Warren Nick, Middlesex, England.
Warwick University, England.
Wheeldon C, Nottingham, England.
Weidman Scott, California, USA.
Wharton W.D., Northants, England.
Wolff Camille, Grey House Books, London, England.